The Earth Beneath

The Earth Beneath

A critical guide to green theology

Ian Ball, Margaret Goodall,
Clare Palmer and John Reader (editors)

First published in Great Britain 1992
SPCK
Holy Trinity Church
Marylebone Road
London NW1 4DU

British Library Cataloguing-in-Publication Data

CIP data for this book is available from
the British Library

ISBN 0-281-04601-8

Typeset by Pioneer Associates, Perthshire
Printed in Great Britain by
Biddles Ltd, Guildford and Kings Lynn

Contents

Contents

Contributors

Ian Ball. Head of Religious Education at Bishop's Castle Community College and a member of the Shropshire Standing Advisory Council on Religious Education.

Richard Beaumond. Head of Drama and Arts Co-ordinator at Bishop's Castle Community College.

Lindsay Brown. Artist working with community groups by combining art and psychotherapy.

Ian Carter. Anglican chaplain at Liverpool University.

Margaret Goodall. Methodist minister at Newport Pagnell in the Milton Keynes circuit.

Robin Grove-White. Director of the Centre for the Study of Environmental Change at Lancaster University. Formerly Director of the Council for the Protection of Rural England and a member of the Archbishop's Commission on Rural Areas.

Clare Palmer. Research student at The Queen's College, Oxford and teaching theology at Westminster College, Oxford.

John Reader. Director of Pastoral Theology at Salisbury and Wells Theological College.

Introduction

What has Christianity to offer to the current debate on the environment? That is the question which led to this book. It is clear from the recent deluge of literature on this issue that there are many who believe that Christians *do* have something distinctive to say. The sources of guidance and inspiration available, the Bible and the whole history and traditions of the church through the ages, surely have something to tell us about humanity's relationships with the natural world. There is the Christian doctrine of creation to be drawn upon. Are Christians not bound to see the environment as an issue upon which they have a distinctive perspective? These are reasonable suppositions and it is right that a Christian response to the environment debate has begun.

The contributors to this book believe that there is a level to this response that has yet to be considered. So far, the environment debate has been taken at face value: the issue has been the way in which humans are treating the natural world. We want to suggest that there is more to it than this. Beneath the surface is a question about the identity of humanity itself. What are we meant to be and to become? Where does humanity fit into the total picture of creation? Concern for the environment has become one contemporary focus for these questions.

In order to create a forum for the discussion of this issue a conference was organised. This took place at Ripon

1

College, Cuddesdon in September 1990. Not all those who took part have contributed to this book, but they were a part of the process of opening up the debate further. We would like to thank them and indeed the College for making the conference possible. Some of the papers delivered at the conference were subsequently developed into articles which appear in this book. The approach which we adopted both for the conference and for the book was collaborative and inter-disciplinary. Behind this lies the conviction that progress in this area of human concern is more likely to come through a process of open discussion in which a range of views can be expressed, rather than from a dogmatic statement of party responses. This can create a debate where the edges are sometimes a little blurred. However, this is an essential part of the process.

It is hoped that this book will enable others, both Christians concerned with the issues and environmentalists curious about religion, to discover enough common ground to engage in a much deeper discussion. Neither side possesses all the answers, but both have a contribution to make. Part of this process is to examine some of the ideas and thinkers now being utilized for the immediate Christian response in order to raise critical questions about their adequacy for the task in hand. However, it is also important to give examples of ways in which people have already begun to respond at that deeper level so that the discussion may lead into practical activity. If the real question is that of human identity, what can we do about it?

Thus the final section of the book offers examples of grassroots action, some of it church related, some of it not, which can give people ways in, ideas that can be adapted to other situations. Most of the more theoretical material in the earlier sections originated from the direct involvement of the contributors in national or local environmental issues. They represent attempts to think out the nature of that practical engagement in the light of the traditions and resources available to us. The ideas are only of use if they serve to illuminate what is going on at the level of experience. In that sense theory is subordinate to practice. We hope that our attempts to think this through will be instructive for others and that the ideas we offer will stimulate further discussion.

In the first article, Robin Grove-White of Lancaster University points out that it has been the environmental pressure groups who have been responsible for placing this issue on the political agenda. The same can surely be said of how the issue has been brought to the attention of Christians. Once the issues have gained credibility and respectability, they tend to be redefined in terms familiar and non-threatening to both political and religious establishments. Thus part of the political response has been to view the problem as essentially susceptible to economic and scientific solutions. The irony is that this denies the very fact that environmental movements are a reaction against the pressure to reduce life to the frameworks of economics and science. They are a challenge to that limiting way of looking at the world.

Religious responses are subject to a parallel danger. To return to the apparently safe ground of Scripture and tradition conceals the fact that it has been interpretations of those that have been used by Christians to legitimate unacceptable approaches to the natural world. Hence the discussion about the meaning of 'dominion' in the book of Genesis. Simply to reclaim those contentious terms as if they had been environmentally-friendly all along surely lacks integrity and cannot wipe away the memory or the consequences of generations of inappropriate behaviour. To pretend that Christianity has been green all along but has somehow not 'realized' it looks like self-justification rather than a real attempt to acknowledge our complicity in the destruction of earth's resources and to join the struggle for new ways forward.

3

Another consequence of this domestication of the debate is that it limits the *radical* nature of the challenge being launched by environmental groups. It is far easier and safer to try to contain the challenge of 'green' theology within existing boundaries than to be open to the possibility that what it really requires is a complete re-think of traditional Christian attitudes. It is our argument in this book that most of the material that has been published so far has gone for the safe option, that of reinterpreting our existing language. We will suggest that what is needed is something new and as yet undeveloped. If Christians are to share in that process of development they will need to stand much closer to those already moving in this direction and be prepared to let go of ideas from the past that are no longer adequate.

The book falls into three inter-related sections. Part One looks more closely at the question of what is going on beneath the surface of the environmental debate. Robin Grove-White highlights the human concerns about our increasing dependence upon science and technology, the dangers that this carries with it and the resulting anxiety that has surfaced through the environmental movements. He argues that if governments and research programmes fail to address this dimension of the debate it will lead to greater confusion over appropriate responses, and under-mine political solutions. It is the understanding of what it is to be a human being which underlies these limiting approaches and which could be challenged by alternative Christian insights.

Margaret Goodall and John Reader then expand upon this argument. They offer examples of how this anxiety and uncertainty is present both in concern for community life and in current attitudes towards death. Part of the pressure to consume which is so damaging to the planet can be seen as an escape from the question of human identity. We attempt to find our self-worth and meaning in material possessions. We respond to the breakdown of familiar patterns of family and social life by retreating to a past which only perpetuates the injustices and inequalities which mar our relationships with each other and with creation. Christianity must acknowledge its investment in these damaging processes if it is to move forward. Its attitude to women has suggested a pessimism about human nature that fails to offer the necessary hope for the future. At the other extreme we find in the New Age movement and in elements of creation spirituality an unwarranted optimism, which suggests that peace and harmony are now upon us and that all will be well with the world if we can only acknowledge it. It seems that of the familiar insights about human nature available within the Christian tradition the ideas of ambiguity and paradox have the most to offer. The struggle to discover what humanity might become is always in danger of being appropriated by the forces it aims to oppose. We must believe in and work towards a better future, but not fool ourselves by equating that with present protest movements, however attractive or challenging they might be. The question of human identity remains open.

Part Two examines some of the attempts to reformulate the Christian tradition and illustrates the limitations of this response. Clare Palmer offers a critique of the model of stewardship which has been used heavily both within the churches and by politicians. She shows that it is difficult to establish a clear-cut biblical concept of stewardship which corresponds to the tasks it is now being used to fulfil in the debate. She also questions whether any possible interpretation of the term is capable of grounding the critical view of relationships between humans and the natural world which now seems to be required. What we do need are new and more appropriate models for this relationship.

Ian Carter considers the question of whether Teilhard de

Chardin's work can contribute towards a contemporary ecological spirituality. Teilhard is one of the thinkers of the previous generation who appears to have been concerned with the issue of our relationship with creation. Is it possible to claim, on the basis of his work, that Christianity has been developing a more radical or sympathetic understanding of the natural world which predates the environmental movement? The essay illustrates that there are problems with such a suggestion. One is Teilhard's own uncritical view of evolution, which appears to suggest that certain elements in creation, both human and non-human, are expendable in the evolutionary process. His thought also lacks an understanding of science itself as a social product which would allow for a more critical engagement with Christianity. It is perhaps difficult to criticize Teilhard for not taking into account ideas that were underdeveloped at that time, but this does illustrate the limitation of dragging even recent Christian thought for appropriate contemporary responses. Some of the questions we are faced with are so new that it is unreasonable to expect much of either Scripture or tradition.

The third essay in this section launches a critical review of the work of Matthew Fox. Fox is emerging as one of the major figures in the development of creation spirituality. In fact, it sometimes seems as though Fox himself has set out to invent it. That his books and lectures are receiving increasing attention in both the United States and Great Britain suggests that those searching for answers have found little else to turn to. He is 'ahead of the game' in that respect, meeting concerns not yet being addressed by the mainstream churches but that are felt by many within them. The particular critique suggested by Margaret Goodall and John Reader is consistent with the major concern of this book, that is that Fox is likely to provide another domesticated version of the debate.

Will Fox's teaching lead to the radical shift of attitude

now required in order to come to terms with the environment crisis? The answer would seem to be, 'No'. As with much of New Age and creation spirituality thought, Fox's writing takes an unjustifiable and unhelpfully optimistic view of humanity. Broken relationships cannot be dealt with by denial, but only by open acknowledgement and a genuine desire for healing. By dismissing a recognition of the shadow side of human nature as 'dualism', Fox preempts this process and risks projecting onto other groups the very failings that are a part of all of us and which must be addressed. The result is theology vulnerable to political manipulation of a damaging nature, hence the need to offer an ideological critique of his work.

Finally in this section, Ian Ball examines some of the most recent Christian offerings from this country on the green debate. *Faith in the Countryside*, the Church of England's report on the future of rural areas, touches upon this theme in its theological contribution, but only in a way that appears to shift all the blame for the environmental crisis onto the Enlightenment. This is a strangely one-sided interpretation of both Enlightenment thought and Christianity and does not promote the contact that needs to take place between the two. The question of the value of returning to Christian sources in an uncritical fashion is posed with reference to books on ecology by Tim Cooper and Ian Bradley. Can new dilemmas for the human race be resolved by simple reference to the past?

This review of representative examples of Christian attempts to formulate an adequate response by reinterpreting existing concepts and ideas, reveals just how seriously we are failing to address the deeper issues. By limiting our contribution in this way we are missing the opportunity to play an important and effective part in the more general task of struggling towards a new human identity.

Part Three of the book suggests ways in which Christians can be part of this process. Margaret Goodall and John Reader draw upon their respective knowledge of personal and political social theory to establish that one of the most important roles that churches can play is that of creating spaces for open discussion of these human concerns. There are examples of this from Eastern Europe, where the local church has often been the major forum for debate and thus a catalyst for change. In Western capitalist countries there are other bodies and groups which are already fulfilling this function, for instance, the New Social Movements, but there are grounds for suggesting that the churches also possess this potential. If this could be released, then they could make a more radical contribution to the environment debate.

The final three chapters give practical examples of how it is possible to create such spaces. Ian Ball describes his experience of leading regular pilgrimages of young people, taking them away from familiar surroundings in order to stimulate new thoughts and ideas, but also to learn about themselves through participating with others in a shared enterprise. This is an educational process in the widest sense, which raises questions about both identity and relationships against the background of a traditional religious activity. Pilgrimage in this context becomes something new, not an attempt to recreate mediaeval times or a Sunday afternoon stroll, but an opportunity to face radical questions about possibilities for the future.

Richard Beaumond explains how local communities can engage in a similar process through community drama. The subject for this may or may not be explicitly environmental, but the same opportunity is there for groups from a particular locality to examine the extent to which their identity rests upon a shared history and to express current concerns in an accessible way. So often the breakthrough in this process of discovery cannot occur until appropriate means of expression are found. The use of music, drama and celebration offers a freedom that can otherwise be confined to those with access to and confidence to employ the written word. In a safe space, created by people themselves for a limited purpose, it is much easier to be open about doubts, questions and conflicts.

In the final chapter, Lindsay Brown, like Ian Ball and Richard Beaumond working from a local base in Shropshire, takes the argument full circle back to the search for identity, as aided by engaging with colour and symbol. This too makes possible the release of feelings and thoughts that cannot often be expressed in language. We can re-establish contact with the parts of ourselves that lie dormant or denied because of past pain or fear. How can there be healing or wholeness of relationships until we learn to acknowledge those aspects of personality which, having been suppressed, are then even more influential on our behaviour at an unconscious level? Getting back into right relationships, with ourselves, each other and the wider creation cannot begin until we can own the broken threads of the past. Only then can we let go with confidence and strike out into an uncertain future.

This locally-based work owes a debt to the vision and encouragement of the diocese of Hereford and its second rural consultation. Although the local projects would have happened anyway, there were those in the churches who could see the potential in them and were prepared to offer both financial and moral support. Here is an example of the church creating space and allowing others to experiment with new ways of working.

In the face of uncertainty, represented to us by, amongst other things, the environment crisis, the normal reaction is to retreat into what is known and secure. But this cannot be enough because it is those very areas that are supposed to be known and secure, science, our religious traditions, our own public selves, that have led us to this position and are now brought into question. Where do we go from here and how can we move forward when these familiar thought patterns no longer warrant our uncritical trust? Here is the essential challenge of the environmental debate. We hope that this book will enable others to glimpse this challenge and encourage them to join the risky enterprise of searching for new answers.

John Reader
October 1991

Part One

1

Human Identity and the Environment Crisis

ROBIN GROVE-WHITE

Does Christian insight about the nature of 'the person' have anything distinctive to tell the world about the phenomenon of environmental crisis and concern?

Increasing numbers of theologians – as different in their approaches as Jürgen Moltmann, Claus Westermann, John Cobb, and Sean McDonagh – have offered their thoughts on green questions. These have focused overwhelmingly on the reality of fallen man's recent historical destructiveness towards nature and the need for new attitudes of care, concern and integration – 'stewardship', 'priestliness' and the like – to shape our future relations with the rest of creation.

However, this chapter has a different emphasis. It argues that the 'environment' phenomenon, now so prominent a feature of Western culture, is as much about our sense of what kind of creatures we are – in other words, about new directions in human *self*-understanding – as it is about our fractured relations with an objectified nature 'out there'. It concentrates less on the sense of physical crisis and scientifically-verified destruction on which recent writers have tended to build, and more on the dynamic social and cultural drives which have underpinned popular understanding of such developments in modern complex

13

societies. Christian insights into the nature of the person are of crucial relevance here, for they can throw light on the central importance of the energy and creativity which have characterised public responses – in ways that have gone unrecognised hitherto.

Before embarking on the argument, I should mention some relevant features of my own background. For most of the 1970s and 1980s I was a full-time environmental campaigner, nationally in Britain and internationally in the European Community. This was a demanding and exhilarating period. The intensity of engagement from within tiny, self-financing membership organisations; the dynamism, energy and originality of one's co-workers; the perpetually evolving sense of shared discovery and self-definition; the boundless opportunities for trial and error in real situations in the public arena; and the groping sense of helping crystallize deep cultural currents which were bypassing official institutions – all of these were daily realities, as our activities helped catalyse the phenomenon of public environmental concern with increasing political effectiveness.

As the 1980s developed, there was also intensifying interest in the related moral, philosophical and religious dimensions of these questions. For the most part, these did not preoccupy the activist organizations, though World Wildlife Fund (now the World Wide Fund for Nature) pioneered its own initiatives, with the International Consultancy on Religion, Education and Culture. Increasingly, through initiatives from a range of bodies – amongst them the World Council of Churches, the Ian Ramsey Centre in Oxford, the Archbishop's Commission on Rural Areas, St George's, Windsor and the Board of Social Responsibility of the Church of England – a new theological focus made itself felt. I became involved personally in certain of these initiatives, and played a small role in some of the approaches that emerged. Overwhelmingly these suggested that more sensitivity in mankind's relationship with nature was an urgent necessity, and was underwritten by Christian teaching.

Doubtless this was and is appropriate. But as the discussions continued, I was plagued by a growing recognition that we were addressing only half the story – that the dominant focus on nature 'out there', and man's detached treatment of it, begged many of the questions that had been buried in the tensions and arguments in which I had been involved as an environmental campaigner. Vital social and cultural processes, underlying society's *definition* of the problems, were being neglected, with the result that the full human significance of the environment issue was remaining obscure.

To throw light on this, here are two ways of looking at the environmental phenomenon – one of them representing more-or-less the contemporary orthodoxy, the other more shadowy and emergent. They have common features, and in important respects they are complementary, yet they rest on rather different ways of regarding human beings – and pose important challenges to Christian understanding.

The 'orthodoxy'

In September 1988 Mrs Thatcher, as Prime Minister, made a speech to the Royal Society which put her official imprimatur on the reality of global environmental problems. The speech – and others like it by leaders in both Western and Eastern bloc countries – assisted the consolidation of a broadly agreed political agenda of issues now considered to be 'environmental'.

What features have characterized this consensus? First, and overwhelmingly, the problems are seen as existing objectively in nature, mediated through the natural sciences. Environmental problems are thus regarded as *physical* problems arising from specific human interventions

15

in natural systems; their character and boundaries are, so to speak, given to us from nature, their authenticity guaranteed by natural scientific investigation and confirmation. This being the case, the argument continues, what are now needed are 'solutions', to mitigate these physically identified 'problems' – solutions which may be found in persuasion or regulation, in international agreements or in the application of economic instruments. In each of the international agreements so far established – on chlorofluorocarbons (CFCs), on sea-dumping of industrial wastes, on sulphur dioxide emissions and so on – there are implicit commitments to beliefs about the physical limits of the 'problems', and about the restorative effects of the particular actions agreed for limiting the pollutants in question.

Clearly, the problems highlighted by this 'orthodox' approach are immensely important. The scientific consensus on issues like global climate change and ozone depletion is impressive and alarming: so too is the evidence of accumulations of toxic wastes and other pollutants in our soil and water. Public opinion and the environmental non-governmental organisations (NGOs) are also seen as playing a significant potential role in tackling the problems: while the 'rationality' and 'responsibility' of the NGOs is seen as suspect, because of their supposed partisanship, nevertheless 'solutions' to the principal problems will not come without their co-operation, in helping shape and mobilize public opinion.

This characterisation of the 'orthodox' approach is drawn most immediately from UK experience. The government's White Paper of 1990, 'This Common Inheritance', broadly embodies this view, but variants of it are now influential in most Western countries. The environmental crisis is now defined as a set of identifiable physical problems, some of them acknowledged as deep-rooted in our economic practice and very difficult to address. 'Solving' the most intractable of them, it is suggested, will require major achievements of regulation, fiscal innovation and international diplomacy, as well as goodwill of a kind almost without precedent. There is no time to be lost: partnerships of industrialists, politicians, NGOs and scientists are urgently needed to help develop realistic means to this end.

This understanding of the situation may seem so self-evident, that it may seem odd to question it. However, it is far from adequate as an account of what has been going on. Here are four of its shortcomings.

Trivialisation of the public's role

With its assumption that the key problems are those identifiable by natural scientific investigation, the orthodoxy fails to account convincingly for the startling fact that almost all of the most significant environmental issues, global or domestic, were identified first, not by governments responding to or using 'science', but by poorly resourced non-governmental organisations and sundry individual environmentalists in the period between the late 1960s and early 1980s. Indeed, too often over this period, the role of science and scientists was to patronise so-called 'emotional' and 'irrational' expressions of public environmental concern – on issues much later acknowledged by official scientific bodies and institutions to be indeed genuine and serious. In most of their outlines and much of their detail, the analyses and prescriptions which now increasingly underpin official thinking focus on many of the issues which environmental groups have highlighted since the early 1970s, whether in the fields of transport, agriculture, energy policy or even industrial policy. These groups have challenged the soaring trajectories of industrial society, the inadequacy of present regulatory processes for controlling rampant consumption, and the need for new approaches which recognise and take advantage of the

17

inherently malleable nature of such concepts as 'economic growth' and 'consumer demand'. To a striking extent, the 1970s analyses of UK NGOs like Friends of the Earth, Greenpeace, CPRE and others have been vindicated – right down to such diverse and specific *causes célèbres* as the economics of nuclear power; the need for, and feasibility of, major programmes of energy conservation and improved end-use efficiencies; the arguments against the increasing proliferation of the private car; the links between environmental degradation in Third World countries and poverty and famine; and the impacts on wild flora and fauna of intensive agriculture.

The point of this observation is not to score points by demonstrating the prescience of NGOs compared with governments and their advisers. Rather, it is to ask how a plausible account of this social reality can be derived from the 'orthodox' description of the environmental phenomenon given above. That model sees NGOs and 'public opinion' as essentially emotive and irrational, given to 'unscientific' outbursts. Such organisations are acknowledged to have had social importance, in having helped bring issues to political attention; but, according to the orthodoxy, it has been science, particularly scientific inquiry conducted within an official framework, which has provided the true litmus test for whether or not issues are indeed issues.

The oddity remains. How and why 'the public' (reflected in the NGOs) understood the issues in advance of the arrival of official 'science', or why their 'intuitions' should have resonated so powerfully with wider social attitudes, is not considered a matter of significance, and these days tends to be set to one side in official circles.

Inflation of the role of science

A second shortcoming of the prevailing orthodoxy concerns precisely its view of the authority of the natural sciences,

18

in providing the criteria for what constitutes 'fact' in the environmental domain. Though the recent White Paper and recent international agreements on issues like North Sea pollution have laid new emphasis on the occasional need for action ahead of scientific 'proof' of damage, the so-called 'precautionary principle', the implicit underlying official conception of science remains a positivistic one. That is to say, scientific procedures are held up publicly as providing 'proof' and as therefore able to define and identify 'fact' in this field.

However, growing understanding of the ways in which scientists actually conduct their business undermines this reassuringly solid picture. Far from providing a fixed, objectively verifiable body of knowledge of nature's workings – through privileged access to physical reality – it is becoming clear that science itself is a social construct, a web of conventions, practices, understandings and 'negotiated' indeterminacies.

The corollary is that scientific 'proof' or 'certainty' in the real-world non-laboratory circumstances in which *environmental* science has to be conducted, is a chimera. Uncertainty and indeterminacy in this arena is not simply provisional; it is endemic. Scientists are necessarily as selective in their identification of 'problems', and the relevant parameters that need to be considered, as are individuals or institutions using any other mode of perception or understanding. What is more, society's concerns and the actions of an infinity of other actors are in constant, and unpredictable, flux. This helps explain why it is that controversy is so recurrent in politically sensitive fields in which science is used by official environmental agencies to underwrite inaction or to provide political reassurance. Quite simply, the scope for redefining issues 'scientifically', to embrace ever more new real-world variables, or to refocus the significance attached to those already acknowledged, is virtually infinite. It follows that

19

the same is true also of the scope for criticism and disagreement, over much more fundamental matters than simply whether any specific scientific claim is 'accurate' or not.

So here too, the prevailing orthodoxy is far less robust than it purports to be.

The perverse dominance of 'interests'

A third failing of the orthodoxy lies in its distorted reliance on the notion of 'interests' as *the* central tool for explaining environmental concern or value, and justifying corrective measures. This tendency flows from the conception of the sovereign individual, which has been at the centre of the British liberal political tradition since John Locke; the picturing of most human motivation in terms of interests has been a natural corollary. It now dominates public political discussion of environmental matters in Britain, whether in the form of argument about straightforward conflicts involving individual 'interests', or talk of 'interests' of generations as yet unborn, or advocacy of the 'interests' of other (non-human) species.

There are two objections to this tendency. In the first place, it is simply not true that *all* environmental concern can be characterised appropriately in terms of interests. In my own experience, contrary to appearances, individuals who have most shaped the environmental movement have been drawn together quite as much by openness and a groping sense of shared, or potentially shared, identity – forged against the prevailing social orthodoxy – as by the pursuit of predefined policy objectives. As continental sociologists like Alberto Melucci have recognised, such individuals have been seeking and perhaps finding a better, more fruitful collective engagement with, and exploration of, reality, discovering it through simple human interaction with one another, against a background of tension and argument with the prevailing social ethos. Such processes are of their nature open-ended and indeterminate. They cannot be represented usefully in terms of interests, other than ex post facto, since even the individuals concerned are by definition unable to articulate fully what they are seeking. Indeed, part of their inspiration has lain in discomfort at, and the wish to find alternatives to, precisely the kind of political discourse that is dominated by the 'interests' mentality.

This leads to the second objection. It cannot of course be claimed that environmental concerns do not involve 'interests'. The problem is more that the present dominance of this way of looking at questions of value has developed a self-fulfilling dynamic of its own. NGOs, recognising that this is the discourse in which our political and legal culture now frames issues most comfortably, have tended to reduce what are frequently more inchoate concerns into terms consistent with the discourse, in their pursuit of advantage in controversies over issues as different as nuclear safety, wildlife habitats, Green Belts, and global climate change. But the effect of this is further to reinforce the vocabulary of 'interest'. Like all specialist discourses, it has difficulty in evolving or representing perspectives on reality which do not readily fit its own particular framing.

All of this points to a striking irony – that the supposedly detached and objective language of interests embodies crucially important *normative* commitments. And in environmental controversies, it is frequently encountered – and resented – as a moral rather than a neutrally descriptive discourse – and a thoroughly inadequate one at that.

No place for mystery

The fourth respect in which the present orthodoxy on environmental questions is inadequate, is in its superficial treatment of the mysteriousness and open-endedness of existence itself. There is little sign in the official descriptions of environmental problems or methodologies of the radically unknown character of the future, or of man's place in creation.

The tendency in such exercises to characterize the future so far as possible in terms of sets of familiar and 'predictable' parameters – in which, for example, markets can flourish – places at the centre of public discussion a sterile and deterministic understanding of existence itself. It is a picture in which the indeterminacy, mystery, apparent capriciousness, open-endedness and ambiguity of life acknowledged by the classical philosophers and religious traditions, and the moral challenges these realities present to men and women encountering them in history, are drained of public significance, or at least 'privatised' by being driven to the margins of public culture. Now 'the unknown' in environmental matters is reduced to merely provisional 'scientific' uncertainty or imprecision. Not only does this view lead to serious intellectual error (as sociologists of science have shown), but it also profoundly misrepresents reality.

Indeed, against a contemporary background of fundamental intellectual disagreement about the nature of scientific knowledge and the status of uncertainty, it is at least a reasonable hypothesis that some of the deeper shades of recent 'green' and 'New Age' religiosity are best understood as cultural manifestations, and of just these disagreements. They can be read as creative, if dualistic, reactions against the hubris of dominant modernist expectations of scientific epistemology. They challenge the way in which, in many institutional practices, such expectations dominate not only our social identities and political priorities in the environmental sphere, but also the definition of boundaries between the fixed and the tractable, between man and nature.

Nor are such tensions present only at the rarefied level

of environmental science and policy. More prosaically, the tendency to atomise human experience, and to represent it in 'objective' behavioural terms, leads to a persistent trivialisation of areas of human experience which may in fact bear on the mysterious depths of the individual person's relations with nature and the cosmos. This could be confirmed in discussion with individuals involved in many everyday disputes about land use planning or nature conservation issues.

The persistent political misrepresentation of human experience, of the kind embodied in the conceptions of (positivistically conceived) 'uncertainty', 'amenity' and 'recreation', constitute a form of imposed hegemony, which is not itself subject to choice, other than in terms which, arguably, intensify mistrust in engaged individuals in environmental and other NGOs, with increasingly disruptive and unpredictable political consequences. This results directly from the fact that the concepts – and therefore the models in which they rest – are inadequate for reflecting the full dimensions of felt experience. To be sure, people use, and even manipulate successfully, such reductionist languages. But the consequent mistrust is corrosive. Indeed, as has already been argued, much of the drive behind environmental politics from NGOs (and their resonances with the wider public) has arisen from it.

So far, this chapter has highlighted several ways in which the orthodox approach to the environmental crisis is seriously inadequate. It is unable to account for, or to encompass, key realities of the political and social phenomenon of environmentalism. Nor are these trivial realities: the significance of the worldwide NGO movement; the basis of the social authority of scientific knowledge; the complex character of human purposes and identities in environmental argument; and the need to address authentic human concern about deeper mysteries of existence – these are far from insignificant matters. Yet the orthodox model has little or nothing to say about them.

What emerges from these limitations is something still more deeply disturbing, which has gone largely unrecognised in recent theological discussion of the environmental crisis – that the orthodox description of the phenomenon embodies *a seriously inadequate conception of human nature at its very centre.*

No matter where one looks in the environmental sphere – whether to land use planning law, environmentally-related forecasting tools, appraisal methodologies such as cost-benefit analysis or probabilistic risk assessment, or simply social expectations of the natural sciences – a disturbingly one-dimensional picture of human identity emerges. In it, man is seen as a being whose rationality consists over-whelmingly in his/her capacity to calculate where his/her personal advantage lies; an isolated, atomistic individual always able to know in advance and in isolation, what he/she wants (his/her 'interests'); a being for whom *social* interaction and mutuality are merely means for achieving personal ends, rather than engagements of intrinsic moral importance in their own right; a being whose concern for any deeper mysteries of his or her relationship to reality is devoid of practical or political significance; a being who, through science, has unmediated and unproblematic access (actual or potential) to knowledge of the nature of essential physical reality. It is overwhelmingly a picture of the human person as rational-individualist calculator, whose only authoritative knowledge is that modelled on the natural sciences, positivistically conceived.

Concern about our reliance on such a picture of the human person has been implicit in some of the most seminal critiques in the environmentalist canon over the past twenty-five years. The critiques of E. F. Schumacher, Ivan Illich, Jacques Ellul, and Fritjof Capra were alert to the presence of this distorted picture of the human subject in the forces promoting technological insensitivity and environmental carelessness – for example in the corporations, public and private, producing hugely polluting *effluents*; in agricultural systems reliant on the intensive use of chemical additives and exploitation of animals; in energy systems locked into the pursuit of supposed economies of scale, at the price of more and more environmental damage; and so on. But there has now been a striking new development. Now, disturbingly, the same model of the human subject inspires and shapes the techniques, institutions and methodologies that are being developed to *solve* these very problems. It is conspicuously present in the new environmental economics highlighted in the White Paper of 1990, and in those strains of geographical, legal and political analysis which are now beginning to be applied to environmental problems.

In short, embedded in the methodology of public solutions now being invoked to address environmental problems in industrial countries like the UK is much the same *normative* picture of man, and of human capability, which I am arguing has given rise to much of the political tension about the environment in the first place.

Yet this overall model does have some strengths. It has helped clarify the structure of certain kinds of environmental problems – not least because the relevant social, political and regulatory institutions, being embedded in the same cultural matrix, are framed to respond to the way of looking at problems that the model prescribes. Traffic engineers, economic analysts, risk assessment specialists and the like, operate within much the same assumptions about human behaviour implied by the model, to the good of the limited communities for whom they work. But the wider constraints on thought imposed by the model are still more striking. For it leads to a picture of the overall environmental 'agenda' described at the outset of this chapter, as a set of visible and discrete problems, which present themselves objectively in the form of 'externalities' from economic processes. As we have seen, such a description is achieved only at the cost of dangerous over-simplifications and omissions.

The 'alternative'

Consider now a sharply different hypothesis to that offered by orthodoxy, which explains the way in which environmental issues have become socially defined.

Particular industrial societies like ours have become progressively more locked into a vast range of commitments, which have developed over decades and which are economic, industrial, infrastructural, geopolitical, technological and social. These have been underpinned by, and work to reinforce, a dualistic picture of man and nature. Most of the commitments (to individual motorised mobility, to ever higher levels of energy use, to social, moral and cultural norms encouraging increasing levels of material consumption) have tended to be producer-led. They have been entered into without prior analysis of their cumulative potential impact. They are commitments which help define and shape our collective social and political identities.

These commitments have helped determine the parameters not only of the physical but also of the social domain. Many of the most widely diffused technologies (such as the telephone, and the word-processor) have few obvious disadvantages; but many (such as the internal combustion engine, civil nuclear power, pesticides, and chemicals producing toxic wastes) do have adverse impacts, the significance of which becomes recognised retrospectively, and only gradually and with difficulty. Moreover, the social arrangements needed to make them 'work' (itself a disputable achievement) may be at least as significant, and arguably as negative, as their physical/biological impacts.

In our own time, these social configurations have become

more and more dominant. Crucially, in the societies in which they are present, they have been producing their own distinctive patterns of social anxiety and response. The discourse of 'environmental' problems, expressed in terms of the same man-nature dualism as industrialism itself, is one key manifestation of this. Environmental pressure groups and green parties have derived their (paradoxical) political potency from the fact that they have discovered ways in which particular land use or pollution controversies can be made to symbolise, and resonate with, these widely shared, deeply rooted but previously unarticulated concerns. Not only do they focus on the conspicuous physical dimensions of the changes wrought by the social commitments (as these have become more and more pervasive). But more crucially, they also focus on the increasingly problematic new relationships with the political and regulatory agencies responsible for monitoring what are now effectively scientific experiments imposed on society as a whole, and for providing reassurance that any negative side effects are being kept under control.

It is environmental groups who have helped define the risks and dangers which our society now recognises as part of its description of the 'natural', and this has ensured their credibility with the public at large. It is through social processes like these that the political agenda of environmental concern has become defined. The particular issues on which the agenda is focussed (such as water quality, whales, and wastes) are ultimately arbitrary. The notion that science somehow discovers 'the problems' and then sets an environmental agenda, is frankly naive.

This way of looking at the problematic differs sharply from what I have described as the orthodox way. Moreover, it expresses a quite different understanding of the human being, and it thrusts this understanding into a much more central role in the definition both of environmental 'problems' and the appropriate policy responses.

27

Rather than the environmental agenda being presented to us from on high by science, the actual selection of issues constituting the agenda becomes seen as constructed socially, as a political response to pressures from 'below' – pressures which in turn arise from human beings responding gropingly to a sense of the ways in which their moral, social and physical identities are being threatened and misrepresented in ways they do not fully understand. Because our culture gives greatest recognition to factors defined in objective 'scientific' terms, these anxieties focus most readily on the physical manifestations of these disorders – on individual abuses of or incursions into the 'natural' environment. But it is a game of shadows and mirrors. Arguments at power station public inquiries focus on energy forecasts, not simply as statistical disputes, but as ways of challenging the deterministic conceptions of human behaviour and consumption implied in the econometric equations adopted by the forecasters. Technical arguments about pesticide consumption, apparently focussed on physical safety, challenge the arrogance and reductionism of the regulators' and official scientific advisers' unilateral assumptions about human behaviour in real-world situations. Protests at particular land use developments may be concerned as much with the felt implications for future erosion of communities and social exchange, as with the immediate merits of particular developments seeking particular planning permissions. In these and many other instances, the particular physical 'environmental' schemes in contention resonate with significance, as *prisms* through which deeper implicit arguments about human and social identity can be conducted.

Such an account has two crucial implications. First, it provides a description of the environment problematic as a whole, embracing the four additional dimensions which, I have argued, the orthodox picture omits. Ultimately this is because, second, it rests on a quite different representation of human nature. The sense of unease experienced by those who argue with energy or traffic forecasts, or about regulatory myopia or scientific uncertainties, is social and moral, quite as much as physical. It is now widespread – as the escalating memberships of NGOs, and the unpredictable ebb and flow of green politics, suggest. It arises from a particular, unprecedented set of historical contingencies, in which new configurations of technology and capital, linked to bureaucratic and corporate power, can be seen as presenting societies with a Faustian bargain – goods and 'welfare', in exchange for subtle (and not so subtle) manipulations of man's self-understanding and moral identity. Perhaps the most corrosive dimension of this bargain is the escalating encroachment into sensitive moral and human territory concerning life itself – witness the intensifying conflicts over biotechnologies.

Seen in this light, the importance of understandings of human nature radically different from that embedded in the orthodoxy becomes more and more evident. Take the quite different pictures of the human subject found in classical Greek and Christian thought. These represent humankind in terms both more elevated and more pessimistic than the rational-individualist model. Men and women are seen as aspiring to worthwhile and fulfilling lives in an existential framework of faith, hope and love, as well as profound fear of and respect for the unknown. But they constantly overreach themselves, seduced by the belief that they can be in control. In this framework, rationality consists in, and is directed towards, an ever-clearer recognition of and response to such essential realities. In the seminal Greek and Christian texts, we are offered conceptions of human capability and limitation, which are hugely rich in possibility but within frameworks bounded by 'the nature of things'. Human mischief and misery are never far away. Crucial to these accounts, in their different ways, is the central position of the mysterious and the humanly indeterminate in man's condition. The German-American philosopher Eric Voegelin has provided an account of the historical emergence and subsequent erosion (particularly since the Enlightenment) of such models of human self-understanding (the 'order of being'), in ways which are consistent with contemporary understanding of the sociology of knowledge.

Such a picture of our condition resonates more closely, I suggest, with the contemporary experience of immense numbers of people apparently unconcerned with 'philosophy' or 'the environment', than does the rational-individualist calculator picture. As a corollary, it could be argued that because the liberal pluralist intellectual framework to which we are currently committed is uncomfortable with discussions about unitary visions of human nature, it is through 'the environment' that these tensions in the representation of human self-understanding have been making themselves felt politically.

There are good reasons why 'the environment' has come to play this role – not the least of them being its previously 'uncolonised' character as a political/ideological domain, and the role of the nature/man, science/politics dualisms as a central, structural tension in Western thought.

I have painted this picture in broad terms. It is compatible with most of our current understanding of the most serious 'physical' issues. Indeed, it enhances the impact of natural scientific descriptions of the seriousness of phenomena such as the greenhouse effect and ozone depletion by clarifying the necessary limitations of the epistemological tools used by governments and researchers to define and come to grips with them, thus emphasising the underlying uncertainties in our understanding.

Concluding observations

I have suggested two different ways of conceptualising the contemporary environmental phenomenon – the 'orthodox' account, which lays particular emphasis on positivistic conceptions of scientific understanding and human inclination; and an 'alternative' account, which stresses the central role of human relations and cultural contingency in the emergence of the concerns societies are now coming to label 'environmental'. Are these two descriptions equally valid? Can we choose either one with equal integrity?

The implication of my argument is that we cannot. Indeed, my contention has been that many of the individual controversies that have brought particular elements of the environmental agenda to the surface have arisen in realistic and spontaneous grassroots reaction to the restrictiveness of the dominant 'orthodox' view in our public discourses and institutions. Through intense disputes, frequently 'displaced' so as to be barely recognisable as such, surrounding the positivistic methodologies used by official agencies – cost-benefit analysis, probabilistic risk assessment, decision analyses, and so on – concern about the environment has become an arena in which profoundly important arguments about human identity are now being conducted.

A number of perceptive analysts – Martin Jacques and Paul Morris, for example – have argued that the environment movement can be understood as a vehicle for the reassertion of public, collective values in societies whose individualism has overrun its course. Seen in this context, the phenomenon is one of a number of manifestations of an emerging resistance to the mean and inadequate conceptualisations of ourselves which have become embodied in our public institutions.

Christian thought – and in particular Christian insight into the nature of 'the person' – can make an immense contribution to the understanding of these processes, whilst simultaneously refreshing itself through engagement with crucially important, subterranean currents of contemporary public concern. For the Christian conception of human nature is astonishingly rich. The Greek Orthodox theologian Kallistos Ware reminds us that in Christian tradition,

> the reality of our personhood is far more than any explanation that we choose to give of it. It is an intrinsic feature of personalness to be open, always to point beyond. The human person is that in which new beginnings are continually being made. To be human is to be unpredictable, creative, self-transcending.

At the same time,

> human personhood, like the personhood of God, is exchange, self-giving, reciprocity. As a person, I am what I am only in relation to other persons. My human being is a relational being. My personal unity is fulfilled in community.[1]

A new generation of theologians, such as John Milbank and John Reader, have now begun to explore the implications of post-modern thought for theological understanding of the variety of configurations human values and personality can take within this understanding.

But there is much more of deep significance for our futures. The human dimensions of the environmental phenomenon need to be understood as an arena – perhaps the emblematic arena of our era – in which spontaneous rebellions against institutionalised distortions of the human spirit in our cultures can be discerned and expressed.

Let us conclude with a passage by a good man who does not claim to be a Christian – Vaclav Havel, now the President of Czechoslovakia. In his magnificent 1977 essay,

'The Power of the Powerless', written in response to the repressions of what he calls 'post-totalitarian' Czechoslovak society, Havel goes out of his way to communicate the implications for our own Western cultures of the then deep sickness of his country:

The essential aims of life are present naturally in every person. In everyone there is some longing for humanity's rightful dignity, for moral integrity, for free expression of being and a sense of transcendence over the world of existence. Yet at the same time, each person is capable, to a greater or lesser degree, of coming to terms with living within the lie. Each person somehow succumbs to a profane trivialisation of his or her inherent humanity, and to utilitarianism. In everyone there is some willingness to merge with the anonymous crowd and to flow comfortably along with it down the river of pseudo-life. This is much more than a simple conflict between two identities. It is something far worse: it is a challenge to the very notion of identity itself.

In highly simplified terms, it could be said that the post-totalitarian system has been built on foundations laid by the historical encounter between dictatorship and the consumer society. Is it not true that the far-reaching adaptability to living a lie and the effortless spread of social auto-totality have some connection with the general unwillingness of consumption-oriented people to sacrifice some material certainties for the sake of their own spiritual and moral integrity? With their willingness to surrender higher values when faced with the trivialising temptations of modern civilization? With their vulnerability to the attractions of mass indifference? And in the end, is not the greyness and emptiness of life in the post-totalitarian system only an inflated caricature of modern life in general? And do we not in fact stand (although in the external measures of civilisation, we are far behind) as a kind of warning to the West, revealing to it its own latent tendencies?

'Latent' tendencies? Should Christian thinkers not recognise in this resonant passage clear pointers to the urgent significance of the environmental critique, as a truly hopeful sign for humanity?

Notes

1. A. Peacocke and G. Gillett, 'The Human Person and the Greek Fathers' in *Persons and Personality* (Blackwell 1987).

2

Environmentalism as the Question of Human Identity

MARGARET GOODALL and JOHN READER

This chapter has been written as a joint response by Margaret Goodall and John Reader to the conference paper given by Robin Grove-White on which the opening chapter is based. As with the later chapter on creating spaces, the writing has been done collaboratively but it will be made clear in this introduction who has been responsible for which sections.

Introduction

Our response to the suggestion that the environment debate conceals an even deeper concern for the question of human identity has been entirely positive. Thus, the first section of this article attempts to expand upon that theme by providing further evidence for this. In particular, we examine the current uncertainty about what it is to be a human being, both some of its causes and some of its consequences. The second section moves on to discuss ways in which the church has failed in practice to do justice to its insights into human nature. Margaret Goodall gives examples of an overly pessimistic view of humanity, especially as it emerges in the church's attitudes towards women. An emphasis upon failure and guilt can lead to a refusal to acknowledge and affirm the total value of human life and can be used as a means of exercising power over the less fortunate members of a society.

At the other extreme lies an optimism about humanity that borders upon unhealthy romanticism. This is to be found particularly at the moment in the New Age movement and in some elements of creation spirituality. Margaret Goodall reviews some of this material in a critical but balanced way, acknowledging the importance of the questions to which this optimism is a response, but also showing the need for realism. This leads to the issue of where it is now possible to locate a balanced and realistic approach to human identity which leaves scope for the sort of changes which are necessary in order to respond to the environmental questions.

Ontological Insecurity

One of the fascinating insights of sociology is that concern for the environment reflects a deep human insecurity in the face of the growing complexity and uncertainty of society. Although our relationship with the natural world is the explicit issue, what is really at stake beneath the surface is humanity's understanding of its place within the whole. The real question is, 'What is it to be a human being?'

What are the causes of this insecurity? First, the West has seen the breakdown of what might be called universal world views, including those of the various religions. The very encounter with other faiths and other traditions has challenged the claims of any one of them to offer a definitive understanding of existence. Those who now make exclusive claims to have the monopoly of truth are rightly treated with suspicion. This is not merely a matter of philosophy but also of practical politics. This century has seen the death of millions of people at the hands of totalitarian regimes which have claimed to possess the truth. Thanks to the masters of suspicion, Marx, Freud, Nietzsche and more latterly Foucault, we are acutely aware of the irrational forces which lie beneath the surface of all claims to have established a rational explanation of and approach to reality. Marx saw the economic forces at work, Freud the powers of the unconscious, Nietzsche the will to power and Foucault the power operating within different discourses, even those of the human and natural sciences. It is now increasingly difficult to argue that any one position provides a neutral ground from which to make judgements of the others – although this has always been an essential part of the Enlightenment project.

Add to this the rapid pace of change of contemporary industrial society and the consequent breakdown of familiar patterns of social life, community and family and we are faced with a humanity uncertain of both its role and its future. We are all at sea in an open boat and, even worse, nobody's boat looks more secure than anybody else's. Christianity too has been afflicted with this radical pluralism.

First of all, it is clear that the Christian tradition has all too often been used as a legitimation for the unjust exercise of power, as a means of social control. This is a constant danger. Even now the Conservative party wishes to use it as an influence for its own social policies, to restore moral fibre within the nation. One might say that environmentalists also are attempting to appropriate the tradition, although they wish to turn it green, not blue. So, Christians must remain on constant guard against such potential ideological uses of their tradition by those who claim to be inside it. We must have our own ideology critique and be ever suspicious of universal claims.

Second, it is plain that the Christian tradition is itself far from being united or uniform. If anyone states that, 'the tradition says this . . .' it is legitimate to ask, 'Which part of the tradition?' No one individual or group can claim to speak for all on any matter of doctrinal significance, which must of course include understandings of what it is to be human. It would not take too much research to establish that Christian tradition has given a number of different and even conflicting answers to that very question over a period of time. There is no one Christian answer to the question of what it is to be human, any more than there is to the question of the nature of God.

Christianity is deliberately vague on moral issues to allow it to be utilized as part of any ideology critique. If it offered too specific a content to answer such practical questions it would limit its effectiveness as a critical agent, as a force for change. It is thin on content but forceful in its vision. If this is so, then it is not going to provide detailed answers to the ecological questions, but it will provide a sense that there should be something more to life than material prosperity or economic survival. What that 'more' is, will be a matter of debate even within the tradition.

The Person

William Temple said, 'I am greater than the stars, for I know that they are there and they do not know that I am down here'.[1] This ability of humans to have knowledge of things other than themselves has enabled them to go beyond the level of existing to that of examining the meaning of life and of their place and purpose in it. We know that we shall die, but it is this search for the meaning of life, given that there is pain and death, that has prompted humanity to look for something beyond itself. There must be a reason for our ability to see beyond our immediate needs. We cannot believe that this is all there is, that we are nothing but a naked ape or an accidental collection of atoms. Life is too short for all that there is to learn or experience. This being the case, it is easy to see why the idea of re-incarnation is popular, being believed by one third to a half of the world's population, even by children who profess no other religious beliefs.

The transience of human life leads us to try to distance ourselves from death. Society does not know how to handle death, so the 'with sympathy' cards are ambiguous in their phraseology, discreetly expressed so as not to offend. While politics, sex and to some degree religion, have become accepted subjects of conversation, that of death remains a taboo. This would seem to suggest that to most people the area is too painful. Having come to terms with their own mortality, they do not wish to be reminded of it by contact with another's death. America leads the way in many social trends, and it is interesting to note that there undertakers are becoming known as 'thanatologists', a word which has no obvious connection with death, unless you happen to have a knowledge of Greek!

It is against these odds that humanity has sought to discover its identity. The creation narrative ends with Adam and Eve being thrown out of the Garden because they have sinned. Even this picture of God's perfect creation incorporates the realisation that humanity is broken. We have all sinned and become a part of our own destruction. It is impossible to describe ourselves as human without reference to what is wrong with us, or without an awareness of broken relationships, of why we are unhappy, or of why we fail. The reasons for this brokenness were important to the writers of the Old Testament and the explanation given in Genesis for the expulsion from the Garden was that man had tried to be like God, having all knowledge. As a result we have created a gap between ourselves and the rest of creation. If we recognise that we have been broken by our actions towards ourselves and others, just as creation has been broken by our humanity, and if we look to find reconciliation within ourselves, then we will begin the reconciliation of the whole of creation. The Genesis story shows humanity being called good as a part of the natural world; and people, reflecting the Trinity in whose image they are made, are created in relationship. Being truly human is not about independence but interdependence, with each other and the rest of the created world. In the Garden of Eden man was given dominion over what had been created, but not the right to tyrannize, ruin or exterminate. Without this attitude of responsibility, humanity has no dignity.

In an attempt to make ourselves immortal, to avoid the reality of death, we surround ourselves with material things and in so doing we are killing the planet by our use of finite resources. Ownership is all that many understand. They look for life's meaning in possessions and use inanimate objects to tell others who they are. Clothes with the name Dior or Gucci are worn to signal that the wearer has judgement, style and personality. 'You are what you buy,' is a common theme. Many parents will have found that, having children at a primary school with no uniform, even their young children are under pressure to conform because they 'have a reputation to keep up' and their 'street cred' is dependent on their clothes or hairstyle. We are even in danger of turning the environmental movement into a cult. Unsliced wholemeal bread which has not been expensively purified costs more than the sliced, bleached loaf. We are encouraged to buy water in bottles, to have ionizers instead of air fresheners and to buy all kinds of environmentally-friendly things. But the pressure is still to buy, to possess. The ideology of consumerism is ingrained in Western culture.

Jesus' pattern of life was to live 'lightly'. He charged his disciples to take nothing with them (Luke 9.1–6). Many times he pointed out the dangers of attachment to wealth, possessions and power, all things which we use to help us evade the question, 'What does it mean to be human?' What are we afraid of? Why do we need these things to give our life meaning? Why are we afraid to be left alone with our true selves, preferring the 'acceptable' face we show the world?

There is a need for us to be able to see some result of our actions in order for us to believe in ourselves. The Lent '88 study course sponsored by the Not Strangers But Pilgrims inter-church process was entitled, 'Who On Earth Are You?'[2] The starting point of this series was the reminder that we tend to categorise people, to label them, by their work. (Did you read the list of contributors to this book in the introduction and do the same?) If we have no paid employment then our value as people is diminished; we feel we have nothing to offer. Identity is defined in terms of roles, job, marital status, or economic power. The Protestant work ethic makes us feel guilty if we are not producing and unemployment is seen as a denial of value.[3] Thomas Aquinas defined humans as beings with a brain and hands,[4] but the automation of modern technology has deprived many people of the opportunity to use their brain and hands. So they look to find fulfilment elsewhere.

One way to prove our value and worth is to dominate, either people or non-human areas of creation. This is seen in the language used for nature which has been depicted as the slave of humankind. In line with the position of women in society in the pre-feminist age, the language used in Western forms of speech for nature is that of male domination.[5] Natural resources are exploited, rivers regulated, virgin forests are penetrated, ownerless property is taken over, secrets are wrenched from the bosom of nature. The need to dominate in order to prove that we really do exist comes from a lack of self-worth. Low self-image can either lead to people withdrawing into themselves or needing to have power over others. The church claims to have the answer for this, as in Christ we are all part of his body, with our own unique purpose in him. There is no need for domination as we are all equally loved, and so recognising another's uniqueness is not felt as a denial of our own place. But, as we shall see, the church has not always recognised or affirmed the value of the person. In particular, we need to examine how Christianity has addressed the issue of self-worth. We focus upon its attitude towards women because the hierarchical and patriarchal approach often adopted is so readily transferred to humanity's relationship with the natural world.

Recent sociological research has contributed to our understanding of the problems arising from the increased complexity of modern society. A number of different explanations have been offered for the current emphasis upon questions relating to human identity. The work of Anthony Giddens will be commented upon shortly, but we would also like to draw attention to the contribution of Jürgen Habermas and Alberto Melucci. However, in order to balance the theoretical approach, we offer a specific local example.

While working in Shropshire John was part of a local group which met on a number of occasions to discuss matters of local concern. The group included both locals and newcomers and it was the tension between the two which provided a focus for many of the discussions. Newcomers had moved into the area with the expectation of being able to belong to a close-knit rural community. What they failed to acknowledge was that it was their very presence which posed the greatest threat to the continued existence of that type of community. On the other hand, local people expressed an ambivalence towards the influx of newcomers. While they did bring with them fresh energy and new ideas which could contribute to the greater good, they were also resented because they appeared to take over so many local organisations. The superficial perversity in this approach becomes easier to understand once one grasps that the underlying issue is about the quality of relationships.

To many an outsider the crucial social question in the

area would appear to be that of class. In what has been described as a feudal structure – a strict social and economic hierarchy with high levels of dependence upon key local landowners – the determining factor in community relationships would appear to be that of people being prepared to fit into this hierarchy. However, according to the interpretation of older locals, this was not the case in the past. Unlike contemporary rural society, one's value as a person was not measured by one's status in the social hierarchy or command of economic resources, but in terms of the quality of one's work and the nature of one's contribution to community life. In other words, you might be a humble woodsman living in a tied cottage, but if your work was good and you were involved in local activities you would be held in respect at all levels of local society. It seems as though it is only with the breakdown of these communities that class becomes more of a determining factor.

The key to this change in relationships is personal knowledge of one's fellows. When the communities were still relatively static everybody really did know everybody else and could make their judgements accordingly. There was nowhere to hide, not even for the gentry. Nowadays such a knowledge is not possible. People move into the area, and their background and family history remain unknown if they wish it to be so. They may work elsewhere and can choose whether or not to become involved in local activities and concerns. After a few years they may move on without ever having established close relationships in the locality where they were living. This is the real source of resentment between locals and newcomers: the damage that is done to the quality of relationships by an influx of outsiders who can choose to remain aloof and apart. One member of the group described this as 'a poverty of relationships'.

If it is the case that at least part of our identity is based on our relationships with others, then threats to a familiar network of relationships will lead to a loss of identity. Newcomers to rural life are accustomed to finding their personal identity in a series of unconnected or fragmented contexts – family, work, sports clubs – that depend less and less upon where they actually live. Locals however are used to all aspects of their lives being intimately bound up with the locality and perceive such fragmentation as a threat. The tension between the two groups that results from this becomes a major theme which is symbolised by discussion about the quality of community life.

This is merely one example of what we believe the sociologists are trying to explain and to which the environmental movement may well be a reaction. To turn first of all to Giddens, he believes that non-capitalist societies are geared to traditions in such a way that everyday life is perceived as routine and secure. In other words, it is possible to live one's life within a fairly static environment, knowing what is expected, how to react to situations, what circumstances and people one is likely to encounter and so on. It is the development of capitalist urbanism which eats away at this structure, gradually eroding not only the routines but also the meaning that people can attach to them. Large tracts of activity are denuded of moral significance and become instead matters of economic necessity. This leads to low levels of what R. D. Laing calls 'ontological security', a sense that one's life has coherence and purpose.[6] This then highlights the question of identity. If my life is so fragmented and confused, how do I know who or what I am? An individual may be called upon to play one role with the family, another on the journey to work, yet another at work, a further one with friends on evenings and weekends. The environmental movement has become one contemporary focus for the question about identity arising from this ontological insecurity. It would seem that this is a valuable explanation.

Habermas takes the discussion further within his own distinctive sociological framework.[7] He prefers to describe what is happening as 'the colonisation of the Lifeworld'. 'Lifeworld' is a term derived from the sociology of knowledge, and refers to an unquestioned background of beliefs and assumptions within which one pursues one's life. This has a lot in common with Gidden's notion of the routines of everyday life but does emphasize that such routines can be based upon beliefs and values. What Habermas suggests is that one's Lifeworld continues undisturbed until the forces of fragmentation unleashed by the development of capitalism challenge one's beliefs by showing that there are other possibilities. Suddenly one is forced to see one's beliefs as a matter of choice and this raises the question of how such choices are to be made. From that moment on it is impossible to pretend that one's way of life is the only one possible. This in itself leads to uncertainty and insecurity.

However, the influences of capitalism are even more threatening as, according to Habermas, the very criteria by which decisions about everyday life are made are being challenged. Decisions that were made on the basis of moral values, in terms of quality of relationships, are being turned into issues of economics. What Habermas terms the 'steering media' of money and power characteristic of the systems world of commerce and industry invade the Lifeworld. Within the context of the environmental debate, the issue of humanity's relationship with the natural world becomes increasingly subject to criteria of profitability. 'Going green' becomes a new commercial venture for as long as there is money to be made out of it. The environmental movement is partly a reaction against this pressure and represents a defensive attempt to hold the

MARGARET GOODALL and JOHN READER

boundaries of certain aspects of life against this invasion
of financial considerations. At this stage we do not intend
to examine the validity of Habermas' explanation but
merely to point out that he too believes that there is a
question about identity that at least requires attention.

Melucci emphasizes another aspect of this same question.[8]
In his analysis of New Social Movements (NSMs) he draws
our attention to the fact that human experience is now
often limited to that which can be measured and verified.
Anything which falls outside these boundaries – things
which he says traditionally belonged to the dimension of
the sacred – are not to be taken seriously. NSMs are a
reaction against this attempt to rationalize all aspects of
people's lives. They are a form of collective action which
intends to re-establish certain human experiences as valid
areas for discussion by essentially symbolic means.

Three examples of this can be given. The precarious
nature of youth poses for society the question of time.
Young people have come to act as a cultural symbol,
representing the characteristics of changeability and
temporariness. Their challenges symbolise the right to
turn back the clock and make a fresh start, to question
professional and personal decisions and to measure time in
ways not governed by instrumental rationality. Perhaps
one might want to say something similar about the now
popular notion of a mid-life crisis. That such a concept
now exists gives people the opportunity to start questioning
their lives so far and seriously consider whether there may
in fact be more to life which could be realized by a change
of direction. Becoming involved in issues of peace, justice
or the environment is a practical way of expressing this
dissatisfaction with lives dominated by financial or material
motivation.

The women's movement similarly raises a question
which is of concern to the whole of society; that of how to
communicate with another person and accept the other's

46

difference without repressing differentiation within the relationship of power so established. Women call for the right to be recognized as different, even though it is difficult for them to avoid using the language of dominance to express this. Their struggle represents an issue which is crucial for all groups who are attempting to gain equal recognition. Such recognition is difficult to establish in a society which is obsessed with issues of cost-effectiveness and economic viability.

The third example is the environmental movement itself. The apparent focus is humanity's relationship to nature, including each individual's relationship with his or her immediate natural and social surroundings. Thus the human body as well as the environment itself come to symbolize the question of the limits which should be placed upon the destructive potential of technology. How far should human intervention extend and what room remains for the nature which both surrounds and constitutes us? How can we be clear about our relationship with the natural world until we have at least tackled the question of what it is to be a human being? On one level the environmental movement is an attempt to place this question firmly back upon the agenda.

In due course we will move on to examine the types of answers that have been offered and their relative adequacy. However, at this stage the object has simply been to illustrate the fact that the question of human identity is surfacing at a number of different levels. One possible response is to attempt to deny the question or to sublimate it through the various activities which are ultimately destructive of all our relationships; another is to fight to give it expression through issues which can symbolize this deeper concern. What we now need to consider is how optimistic it is possible to be that the question will be allowed to surface effectively.

The emphasis of the church

Interdependence is only possible through a sharing of resources, material and human. But people fear to share themselves with each other. In his book, *Why am I afraid to tell you who I am*?[9] John Powell offers a reason for this. He says, 'I am afraid to tell you who I am because you may not like who I am – and it's all that I have.' The Christian tradition has not enabled people to find themselves or to relate to others. It has centred on failure and guilt, which we all share, and has offered few practical ways of feeling better about ourselves.

The image of God in us is flawed, but Jesus has set the divine seal on human life. He was not incidentally human, but deliberately and thoroughly. By taking human life into the very Godhead he has hallowed human existence and asserted afresh and for ever the worth and dignity of bearing the image of God. Yet most Christians have been content to accept a low view of what it means to be human; they are but dust, and to dust they will return.

In Genesis 2.8 we read, 'Then the Lord God said, "It is not good for man to be alone."' Being made in the image of God who exists in relationship, means that we are not fully human if we isolate ourselves. We need loving relationships, but most of us live or work in institutions which depersonalise us.

The church had the opportunity to provide a loving environment where people are valued as individuals, but in many instances instead of giving encouragement to enable growth, it has restricted and confined in order to produce what it believed to be the ideal. This is especially true in relation to the way women in the church have been treated.[10] It seems no coincidence that it is the passive form of the verb 'to treat' which is always used, reflecting attitudes to women in the church. There has been a tendency to view things of the spirit as higher and superior, with things of the body as lower and inferior. Men have identified themselves with the spirit, or mind, and have identified women with the body, or matter.

Jesus showed friendship to both men and women. He was not bound by the taboos of the time. He allowed a prostitute to wash and kiss his feet and showed no revulsion at the supposed 'uncleanness' of the woman who had been bleeding for twelve years, when she touched him. For the Jews a menstruating woman was unclean, as was anything she touched and this denial of the normal biological function has bedevilled the church since. Until quite recently, after childbirth a woman had to be 'churched', to cleanse her after the birthing process. What has this said to women? Are they to be ashamed of the biological process which enables the human race to continue?

Jesus chose a woman, Mary Magdelene, to be the first to meet him after the resurrection[10] and a woman of Samaria to be the one to take the 'good news' to the Gentiles.[11] He showed no sign of believing that men were superior, or that they are the only ones to whom certain tasks could be assigned. If Jesus is to show us how we should behave towards each other, if he is our example of what it means to be fully human, then why has the church found itself so torn in the process of acknowledging the place of women in its life? A man in the church is seen as someone who has wrestled with theology and come to an informed decision, while a woman is seen as someone to help with the tea rota or the flower list. The lectionary includes stories of the founders of the faith, but little is included about the contribution of women. If stories are read then it is usually those of Delilah or Jezebel! Not those of Deborah, Tabitha, or Phoebe.

A church Margaret attended recently had an on-going programme which was made available to all the congregation. One of the courses on offer was 'Excelling as a

Woman' which included this quotation: 'If I diligently do all the tasks around my home and meet all the demands that are made on me, then I will fulfil God's plan for me.' Ideals were seen to be those of denying self and producing menu plans in order to be efficient when shopping. The parallel course for men was not 'Excelling as a Man' but, 'Equipping Men for Ministry.'

The creation story in Genesis 1 has male and female created together, to complement each other, not to exist in competition. Genesis 2 has woman being made from the man's rib to show that neither is complete without the other. The ideal God created was that both should live together equally. The idea used to support the subordination of women is that given after the fall. The pastoral epistles and Ephesians are often quoted in support of this, but if the church is God's kingdom on earth then it should exhibit signs of the kingdom, the coming together of all in harmony. In an article in *The Independent* on 24 August 1988 entitled, 'The violent chauvinism that hides behind the Church', the case was cited of a minister who, during a marriage preparation class, insisted that obedience was the main duty of the wife to her husband. When she wondered out loud what would happen when her husband was wrong she was chastised for being 'rebellious'. If a woman complains about her treatment she is asked what she is doing wrong. The tension felt between what society is saying about equal opportunities and what the church practices, shows itself in hidden violence in supposedly Christian families.

Although the Bible promises liberation for women as well as men, the church does not show or offer it. The Church of England is still tearing itself apart in its debate over admitting women to the priesthood. It has to discern if it is the will of the Holy Spirit, or simply the spirit of the age. The first person to be entrusted with the news of the resurrection was a woman, who then went to tell the disciples. If Jesus trusted a woman with this, then why do we find it so difficult? Women have been allowed to preach, but not to have authority. Again it comes down to power, to domination over others. For many men, to be under the authority of a woman would be seen as degrading. Perhaps when more women take their place of leadership in the church we will see more of an enabling ministry, than one of domination.

The calling of the church is to reconciliation. The root of the word 'religion' means 'to rebind',[12] or to bind together. It is a vision of human unity, not of social control. The vision of the church is that it reaches out to those who are alien, different, not that it seeks to dominate because it has to assert itself. The Spirit is the one who is the source of life, promoting unity, strength and creativity. She prompts us to heal what is broken, to re-unite what is separate and recreate the face of the earth.

The search for wholeness

It would seem that the church has failed to put into practice the healing of broken relationships because it has clung to a hierarchical view of humanity. It was men who governed and made decisions and women who were reduced to passive recipients. The close identification of women with nature, that which is to do with feelings and physical being, as contrasted with men, who are supposedly rational beings, leads easily into a similar approach to the natural world. The latter becomes another resource to be used, or a form to be shaped for men's enjoyment. If both women and nature are to be accorded the value appropriate to them as part of God's creation, the hierarchical approach must be abandoned and men must regain a fuller and more realistic vision of themselves. Only then can we begin to move towards greater wholeness. The ambiguity of the New Age movement is that it acknowledges the need for this process to begin but mistakenly tries to pre-empt it by assuming the harmony of relationships that must be the goal of that process.

The climate of the world seems to have changed, not just with global warming in the climatic sense, but with a noticeable change of perspective. There is an awareness that what happens in one part of the world cannot be ignored, but will have an effect whether we like it or not. This was brought home to us by the Chernobyl disaster when Welsh sheep farmers discovered harmful effects of radiation in their own flocks, much later. Being an island did not protect us as it had previously in our history. It woke us up to the idea that the earth is a whole and that we are part of it. With it came an awareness that the relentless pursuit of economic growth or personal wealth was not only spiritually harmful but had disastrous consequences for the planet. Instead of being ready to take up the new challenge of what it means to live in a wider community, religion had become increasingly privatised and individualised, 'tending to degenerate into a formula which would embellish a comfortable life',[13] or into a branch of the entertainment industry. It seemed to have no answers, or even to want to ask the questions necessary to find the answers. When the Church of England did speak about the conditions in the inner cities,[14] it was criticised for becoming involved in politics and talking about things which did not concern it. The accepted view of the church is that it is to be responsible for reminding people of the spiritual aspect of life.

It is the nature of people to need hope. Hopelessness sees the future as a reflection of the present; to most people that had come to mean technological advancement, which had alienated them from each other, the natural world and themselves. There seemed little to be optimistic about and even the church emphasized judgement rather than wholeness. It was into this vacuum that the vision came of valuing the sacredness within ourselves and the natural world. This was an empowering vision which promised to do justice to our humanity and the potentials within us.

We had suffered for too long under limiting images of ourselves and the world, of resources that were finite. But the one resource that was found to be boundless and abundant in all our future was the human spirit. The New Age movement had become the focus for the 'revisioning' of history with the whole meaning of nature, self and civilisation overturned.

The popularity of the New Age is apparent to anyone visiting a bookshop. Shelves in prime positions are stacked with New Age publications, ranging from meditations with the medieval mystics to books on ley lines and tarot cards. In 1988 one in four religious books published was on the occult.[15] Much of the experience of the sacred, of mystery, in the church and in modern life, where science and theology have attempted to demythologize, has been lost. But the deep need within humanity for the spiritual remains and has been recognised in the New Age, which has brought together experiences from the occult, Hinduism, freemasonry, theosophy, astrology and the cults. None of these are new in themselves, but they have now assumed a new degree of respectability.

There has been a desire for community and purpose in the face of meaninglessness and anonymity and a nostalgic looking back to the war years as a time when people forgot about themselves and worked together. The family has become less important and has been defined as a community held together by a television set. Those who have become involved with the New Age believe that they have found an answer to their isolation and a meaning and purpose for their lives.

The attraction and contradiction of the New Age

At its best the New Age redresses the balance, allowing for the good in humanity to be recognised. After all, we were originally created perfect and are encouraged by Jesus to become perfect. It also demands a paradigm shift, a development of a changed or higher consciousness, by which we will discover a new set of values that will put the whole of creation into perspective, with humanity as a part of a larger whole, leading to a new level of integration. There is no longer room in this world for disunity; we are all dependent on each other and the only way the world can be saved from destroying itself is through co-operation, not confrontation. Christianity and Western science are held responsible for bringing us to the brink of disaster. Christianity in the West has been seen as the guiding principle behind the development of our society which is now recognised as being spiritually bankrupt and culturally arrogant. Nature abhors a vacuum and when the available 'spiritual space' is not filled by a higher motivation it will be filled by something lower. So the aim is to seek out the single true religious spirit which is at the heart of all religion. This is a renewal of the entire history of mysticism, based on an awareness of self, of our environment and of spirituality rather than materialism.

All these things are seen to be true and necessary to avoid a global catastrophe. Yet the criticism of the traditional fall/redemption model of spirituality as quoted by Matthew Fox,[16] is that it considers all of nature 'fallen' and does not seek God in nature but inside the individual soul. This may be true of traditional biblical expositors, but there are many ordinary people who believe that 'you are nearer God's heart in a garden than anywhere else on earth.'[17] However we have not remained true to the basis of our creed, that God is the creator and sustainer of all, and that all is of value in him.

The motivation for this new age of transformation to a world of unity is that of rebirth. Spangler[18] says that there is too much fear in the world already, so the motive for change is not that of pessimism or despair, which are images of death, but of birth. It is a positive and optimistic alternative to systems of belief which have already proved their inability to offer hope. Their motto is 'think globally and act locally', with an economy based on an individual's creativity and productivity. It is a reaction to the 'me' decade, in which the concept of the 'real self' was the criterion against which all experience was measured. Growth and personal fulfilment were in fact illusions of liberation and destroyed community by isolating the individual within his own limitations. It was necessary to discover a new vision of who we are, as we had suffered under limiting images, including that of the economic market place with the threat of unemployment as that which destroys human dignity. Being passive and waiting for something to happen was seen as disempowering, while insights gained from feminist issues, holistic medicine, alternative technology and an awareness of ecology have given a glimpse of human potential.

The idea that human beings can make a difference is an empowering one and attractive to those who have felt impotent when faced with decisions that have been made 'on high'. E. F. Schumacher, in his book *Small is Beautiful*, writes that 'everywhere people ask, "What can I actually do?"'[19] He suggests that they must work to put their inner house in order and that guidelines for this cannot be found in science or technology, because values depend on the ends they serve. The birth of a new consciousness which would make humans more at one with the presence of God would enable us to celebrate the sacred within the ordinary. It offers action – that of exploring the sacraments of ordinary daily living – and looks to expand the boundaries which we have placed around God, reminding us that we have often treated others as things, without regard for the holiness within.

However, like other traditions, the New Age has shown that it too has dangers and that its optimistic view of human nature is as likely to fail as the one it tries to replace. David Spangler, in *Rebirth of the Sacred*, acknowledges the dangers of this new way of thinking. He cites Jung, who identified the principle of 'enantiodromia', which is the tendency of human actions and intentions to turn into their opposites. This, he admits, is the cause of distortions of the New Age which he calls the 'shadow of Aquarius',[20] and much of the general awareness of the New Age comes from these distorted views, he claims.

There are those who live out their fantasies of adventure and power, usually of an occult or millenniarist form, under the guise of New Age. It then becomes a place of psychic powers and occult mysteries, which many find attractive and where the search for spiritual power and knowledge apart from God also leads to witchcraft, or wicca, with people wanting to do good through white witchcraft. The use of crystals and other objects thought to possess spiritual powers is common for healing or enlightenment. By attributing magical powers to these we are confining ourselves to the material world instead of setting our spirit free to grow in love and harmony. With these 'aids' the world can become a place of fear and anxiety. To overcome this anxiety and enable them to discern the truth, some use ouija boards, pendulums, astrological charts, tarot cards and other forms of fortune telling. Courses are run in mind control and mind expansion which again centres on ways in which we can transform ourselves. The occult is in some ways a 'mirror-image' of Christian faith in that it also renounces materialism and acknowledges a spiritual world view. For some New Agers this is seen as a proper reconciliation of opposites and a reconciliation with nature, for as everything is part of the whole then nothing can be excluded – all is equally valid as a way of experiencing the New Age. It all seems a far cry from the era of the hippies who simply wanted love and peace. Now it seems to have become big business.

A new image of humanity

The idea of God within has become distorted to mean that we are God. In our quest for limitlessness we imagine ourselves as creator instead of co-creator. If we were 'creator', then we could only create forms in our own image, and transformation would be less possible. We become bound by our own imagination. The idea of God within us must be balanced by a living experience of God as the one who is beyond us, or he will become an idol, made in the image of our own personalities. Then we would be even more limited than before.

We have to remember that we are creatures, created by God, and creatures have limits. As discriminating creatures we have to recognise our limits; indeed, it is within these that true freedom lies. Christian faith, as the ministry of Jesus shows, is deeply concerned with wholeness – the restoration of the whole person. But this involves cost. The needs we recognise in ourselves are not met by finding harmony within, but by confronting disharmony. Recognising our own failings is part of the process of growth. If the New Age does not recognise good and evil as separate and says that there is no sin, then we will find it difficult – if not impossible – to grow. As there is no sin, there is no need of forgiveness or mercy; there is only the hope, or the fear, of a higher or lower form of life after reincarnation.

Growth is seen as a 'rebirthing', with people being reborn into new life cycles. The consequences are felt in this life and the next, and the next, but karma has no final judgement. The assumption that whatever conditions we find ourselves in are the result of a past life, can lead to an unwillingness to interfere with another's destiny and even to a lack of concern for the needs of others; it can lead to confusion when facing simple moral choices. But the idea that we are responsible for our own destiny is inviting. We are a people 'come of age' and so can answer for ourselves. To Christians, death means new life. One paradox revealed in the gospels is that if we seek to save our life we will lose it, but by losing it we will gain eternal life.

In New Age thought, God is imagined as an energy or force of which the whole universe consists, not the personal God of the Judaeo-Christian tradition. There is no God to have a relationship with because we are part of the creative energy. Gone is the ambiguity of God being in us and yet apart from us, immanent yet transcendent. Yet our potential is only fully realised when we submit ourselves to God, not when we reduce God to the level of our understanding, because no human path can contain all of God's possible truth. To speak of God is to speak of a mystery. When all the scientists, philosophers, theologians and artists have said all they are able to say there still remains something unsaid. We are promised that we can know God, yet there will always be something unknowable. Without this paradox God becomes something that can be controlled, abused or manipulated; religion withers when it becomes domesticated.

Living with paradox

Humanity is looking for clear answers to the question of its identity and of how we should relate to each other and the rest of creation, so the lack of paradox in the New Age is inviting. Any hint of this paradox is seen by some New Agers as 'dualism',[21] including that of body and soul, God and humanity, humanity and nature, which must be avoided at all costs.

All areas of life are being influenced by these ideas. It is becoming generally acknowledged, for example, that for too long we have put into separate compartments ideas relating to the body and the soul. In a BBC Radio 4 broadcast, 'Music Weekly', on 4 December 1990 the Guildhall School of Music was reported as having changed its courses to enable students to use meditation and improvisation techniques, so that their musical education might become more holistic. This has become a tag on which much is now marketed. The promise is that meditation will unblock channels in the body so that life energy can circulate fully, promoting good health and spiritual awareness.

Just as the Christian tradition limited the possibilities of human potential by a strict world view, so the New Agers are doing a similar thing but from the other end of the spectrum. Both are limiting the nature of God and his ability to work in his world. One by denying the things of the body, of the emotions, which are distrusted and of the material world, which are all seen as unworthy of him. The other by saying that God–consciousness can only be found in ecstasies, in all those things that the Puritans warned against: the arts, dance, music, natural beauty and lovemaking; and that the emotions are central to any revelation.

People are a mixture of mind, body and soul, all of which have needs. The Christian tradition had a low view of humanity and saw the necessity for salvation, while those involved in the New Age have a romantic view, believing that humanity can save itself. The truth is somewhere between, in retaining the tension in our understanding of a God who is both transcendent and yet within us. The model of the cross is that of four points reaching out while the centre remains fixed. We can never fully know the answer to our question of what it means to be human, but the important thing is that the question is kept in focus so that every new model of humanity can be assessed.

Holding on to the Paradox

If it is possible to acknowledge that the New Age movement is raising questions that the churches are failing to address then we can begin to understand the nature of the task now facing the Christian tradition. It will no longer do simply to retreat to safe and familiar statements about humanity that have characterized the Christian response. It is not so much that the churches are not effective in presenting their beliefs, it is more that those beliefs do not articulate the needs and feelings of many people in the face of the uncertainties of modern life. Everything is now open to discussion and can become a subject for further exploration, including the question of what it is to be a human being. The issue for Christianity is not, then, that of what answers it might have to offer, but rather that of whether or not it is willing to abandon its former certainties and join the hunt for new possibilities. Can it engage in what we might term 'the human enterprise' – discovering what we might become?

The only clear guideline is the importance of retaining a balance between reason and emotion, between the head and the heart. The Enlightenment hope for a human reason that would bring an end to suffering and injustice has been discredited, but to abandon humanity to its instinctive or unconscious drives is to let the barbarians back through the gates. On the other hand, the vision of a humanity at peace with itself and the world now in vogue amongst the romantics of the New Age, creation spirituality and idealistic environmentalists seems no more than empty wish-fulfilment, unless it can be balanced by rational thought and political realism. There must be ways of drawing upon both traditions to which Christians can make a contribution.

Perhaps the starting point for this must be a recognition by Christians that they are only one small part of this human enterprise. Their claims to interpret the whole need to be placed in perspective. Nobody can have the complete picture. To deny that is to forego the opportunity of making a contribution to the search. Can we let go of the rails of the Titanic before it slips beneath the surface and join the rest in the lifeboats? Why go down with the ship when it is so obviously doomed?

We would like to conclude this chapter by suggesting that some Christians have already begun this process and that their actions are paralleled by others on the same journey. Here, we believe, are to be found signs of hope.

The most exciting developments appear to be in the New Social Movements – the peace movement, feminism, the environmental groups themselves, plus local groups working to meet needs and combat withdrawal of resources.[22] One can see parallels between their ways of operating and their issues and those emerging from what are called contextual theologies – liberation theology, black theology, minjung theology, local theology, feminist theology. For instance, both sets utilize critical social analysis, work on the margins of institutional life and create new public spaces for debate about matters of moral concern. They acknowledge the value of networking and of employing less formal means of organization; attempt to bring power relations to the surface where they can be openly challenged; and are searching for new and appropriate ways of expressing current human concerns. It is surely no coincidence that their work tends to focus on the needs of minority groups and attempts to gain a hearing for those who fall victim to political and economic developments. It is here that the search goes on for both new forms of social and personal identity.[23]

61

What is the potential of such movements? Charles Elliott, in his analysis of Christianity in the United States,[24] suggests that Christianity falls into three categories: the religion of reaction, of accommodation and of resistance. The first legitimizes the status quo, the second espouses moderate reform and the third works for radical change. We must be clear that this third possibility is only one strand within the whole, and is perhaps doomed to be peripheral. Yet this may be one of its strengths, for then it can act as a constant critique of both institutionalized religion and of abuses of power within society.

New Social Movements share the same ambiguous potential. On one level they are largely defensive, attempting to defend areas of life from the further encroachment of economic values. However, they can initiate a process of emancipation as an educational movement, setting examples of alternative approaches to organization and of human responses to the natural world. They are a focus for questions about meaning and purpose which have nowhere else to surface outside religious circles and may lead to a shift of attitudes.

There are, however, two related dangers for both sets of movements. First, will they just be swallowed up by the existing power structures as they come closer to institutional life in order to implement their ideas? Will they have to compromise too much of their programmes in order to gain a hearing? Second, how can they prevent the networks of power which they aim to oppose operating within their own relationships? Is there finally any escape from the inequalities, injustices and distortions of communication which beset human life? It would seem that the picture is one of continued ambiguity. There is genuine potential for change, but always the danger of other forces taking control.

So we return to the notions of paradox and ambiguity central to the Christian understanding of humanity. There is indeed hope, but it must always be tempered by the knowledge that its ideas and movements can be appropriated by the very agents and structures it is working to change. This is no excuse for inaction, but is a realistic perspective on the effectiveness of action. There are always gaps, opportunities and spaces opening up ahead provided that we have the courage to move into them, but as soon as these become too obvious to others, they will begin to be blocked and closed down. The human enterprise, of which Christianity is a part, demands that we keep moving on into an uncertain but creative future.

Notes

1. William Neil, *Concise Dictionary of Religious Quotations* (Mowbrays 1975), p. 115.
2. Not Strangers but Pilgrims, 'Who On Earth Are You?' (British Council of Churches 1987), p. 15.
3. Ronald Preston, *The Future of Christian Ethics* (SCM Press 1987), ch. 7.
4. E. F. Schumacher, *Small is Beautiful* (Blond & Briggs 1973), p. 139.
5. Jürgen Moltmann, *Creating a Just Future* (SCM Press 1989), p. 55.
6. R. D. Laing, quoted by Anthony Giddens, *A Contemporary Critique of Historical Materialism*, vol. 1 (Macmillan 1981), p. 11.
7. Jürgen Habermas, *Theory of Communicative Action*, vol. 2 (Polity Press 1988), p. 391ff.
8. Alberto Melucci, *Nomads of the Present* (Hutchinson Radius 1989), p. 109ff.
9. John Powell, *Why am I Afraid to Tell you Who I am?* (Collins 1969), p. 12.
10. Kathleen Fischer, *Women at the Well* (SPCK 1989), p. 75ff.
11. Fischer, p. 30.
12. Parker Palmer, *Company of Strangers* (New York, Crossroad 1989), p. 22.
13. Alfred North Whitehead, *Science and the Modern World* (Macmillan 1927), p. 269.
14. Report of the Archbishop of Canterbury's Commission on Urban Priority Areas, 'Faith in the City' (Church House Publishing 1985).

15. Cole, Graham, Higton, Lewis, *What is the New Age?* (Hodder & Stoughton 1990).
16. Matthew Fox, *Original Blessing* (Santa Fe, NM, Bear & Co. 1983), p. 316.
17. Neil, p. 41.
18. David Spangler, *The Rebirth of the Sacred* (Gateway Books 1984).
19. Schumacher, p. 288.
20. Spangler, p. 153.
21. Fox, p. 317.
22. Habermas, p. 393.
23. John Reader, 'Local Theology and the New Social Movements', *Modern Churchman*, vol. 32, no. 4, 1991.
24. Charles Elliott, *Sword and Spirit* (BBC Books and Marshall Pickering 1988), pp. 197–220.

Part Two

Stewardship: A Case Study in Environmental Ethics

CLARE PALMER

There is no doubt that over the last couple of decades awareness of environmental problems has been growing worldwide. Correspondingly, there has been the recognition that, for those of us in the industrialized West at least, a different language is needed with which to speak about the place of humanity in the natural world.

The search for this new language and conceptuality is difficult and complex, yet fundamental to the way in which humans act in the world. One particular danger of such a search is the tendency to latch on to already existing, familiar concepts which seem at first glance to solve the problem. In fact, these terms may act as blinkers which block out deeper consideration of the question at issue.

It is this which I am suggesting has happened with the widespread adoption of 'stewardship' to express the relation of humans with the rest of the natural world. The description of humans as 'stewards' of nature recurs throughout both secular and religious discussion about the environment. Chris Patten MP, when Secretary of State for the Environment, commented in an interview in *The Guardian*: 'It's not just a case of bolting on concern for the environment just because it's the flavour of the month or

the year. It's a matter of trying to change fairly fundamentally the way you look at things.' What is his
proposition for change? He goes on to say, 'I actually think
that the best moral case for a pro-active environmental
policy is trusteeship and stewardship.'[1]

This view is found even more widely among Christian
writers. Pope John Paul II spoke of human 'stewardship
over nature' in 1985. The Church of England General
Synod in July 1990 called for a statement on 'Christian
stewardship in relation to the whole of creation to engage
in a critical view of human responsibility to the living
environment.' For many, both Christian and non-Christian,
stewardship, it seems, has solved the problem of re-
examining the way in which humans relate to the rest of
the natural world. I want to suggest that this is not the
case, and that the use of stewardship can represent an
easy retreat to a comfortable concept which avoids coming
to terms with deeper philosophical and theological issues
inextricably interwoven with the environmental crisis.

Before embarking on this examination, I would like to
add several caveats. I am not intending to suggest that the
use of the term 'stewardship' is homogeneous. Clearly
stewardship can mean different things in different circumstances, the most obvious difference being between
religious and secular discourse. It may be used with an
unspoken biblical, historical or practical association, or
even so generally that it has none of these. I want to
consider some of the most important associations which lie
behind the concept of stewardship (an investigation that,
unfortunately, cannot hope to be exhaustive.) I do not
intend to suggest by this that stewardship could not be
used without intending these associations, or that its use
has never been positive. I do wish to suggest that it is
inadequate, and that the context from which it arises is an
inappropriate one when considering the place of humanity
in the natural world at the present time.

The concept of stewardship in the
Old and New Testament

The concept of human stewardship of nature is frequently assumed to have a biblical foundation, and thus to carry particular authority. However, that this is so is by no means certain. When looking at stewardship in biblical writings, there are three areas which need to be considered: first, the use of the term *steward*; second, whether an attitude which might be described as stewardship of nature is advocated or displayed, and third, if this is the case, whether it is found universally throughout the Bible.

In the Old Testament, the term translated *steward* usually refers to 'the man over the house', with responsibility to the master for the affairs of the household and his possessions, such as in Daniel 1.11. This is frequently also the meaning in the New Testament, but of particular significance here are the stewards in three of Jesus' parables. It is from these that the concept of stewardship is usually deduced. These parables contain three elements – the master, the steward, and the master's possessions or household, for which the steward is responsible. The focus is upon the relationship of the master to the steward. The 'possession' or 'household' of the master is not important in itself, but only inasmuch as the steward must obey and be faithful to the master with respect to it. It is important to notice that nowhere in the Bible is humanity actually described as a steward of the natural world. In this, more precise sense, there is no 'biblical concept of stewardship of nature'.

Considered in a broader sense there are occasions where humanity's position in nature could be described as a kind of stewardship. In Genesis 2, for instance, Adam is told to dress and keep the garden. The idea of Adam tending the natural world as a garden sounds like stewardship, inasmuch as he is responsible for its welfare and fertility.

Yet on closer inspection, it must be said that Adam is, in this story, a rather singular gardener. The contents of the garden seem to have been chosen for the gardener's pleasure; and the animals created solely to keep him company. This elevates humans to a position where *steward* seems a rather inappropriate expression.

Even if Genesis 2 is accepted as portraying humans as stewards of nature, there are many other places where stewardship would be an inappropriate expression. One significant passage concerning humanity's relationship with nature may be found in Job 38 — 41, God's reply to Job out of the whirlwind. Here, God is 'watering a land where no man lives, a desert with no-one in it.' God is directly involved with the land and has no gardener. Humanity is irrelevant. Its position is neither to have dominion over the land, nor to tend and dress it. The 'desolate wasteland sprouts with grass' without human aid. The animals are also completely independent of humanity: the hawk, the mountain goats, the wild ox, the leviathan; they are not made for humanity, not made to be human companions, nor even made with humans in mind. They live their own lives.

From this brief survey, several important conclusions can be drawn. There is no single attitude to the natural world in the Old and New Testament as different perspectives and historical periods are represented. Even if we were to accept that Genesis 2, for example, put forward something we could happily call stewardship, other passages, like the one in Job, suggest a completely different perspective. There is, therefore, a danger in speaking of a 'biblical concept of stewardship of nature'; it is by no means clear that there is one, and even if there were, it would only represent one view of many displayed in biblical writing.

To return, then, in conclusion, to my original three points: first, the actual term steward is never used in association with nature; second, there are attitudes in Genesis which have some resemblance to the idea of 'stewardship' but which do not share all its characteristics; and third, different writers demonstrate a very different understanding of humanity's position in the natural world.

This all serves to demonstrate that the associations frequently made between the idea of 'stewardship of nature' and the Bible are misplaced. Claiming a biblical pedigree for the idea is at best to oversimplify, and may be largely mistaken. It raises the question of why stewardship of nature is so popular among Christian writers, given the lack of actual biblical support for it.

Stewardship in contemporary use

Part of the explanation for the popularity of the idea of stewardship of nature may stem from the upsurge in the use of the term 'stewardship' in the 1950s and 1960s. At this time stewardship came to the forefront of the churches' campaigns for more resources, largely of money but also of time and talents. (The emphasis on talents may be due to the entirely fortuitous coincidence of translation that the unit of money, the talent, found particularly in the parable of the three servants, is rendered in English to mean something rather different). *The Christian Century*, for instance, on 22 November 1950 claims: 'There is only one legitimate answer to the financial problem . . . to . . . teach our people to practice [sic] Christian stewardship.'

Stewardship campaigns took place in many churches, particularly among Methodists and Anglicans; stewardship advisors were appointed in dioceses and districts. All of these focused on the need to recognize that neither money nor time belonged to humanity, but were ultimately God's, and man was responsible to God to make the best use of them. One typical definition of stewardship of this sort is the following:

We use the word steward in the biblical sense, as a person who has custody of someone else's resources and is responsible not only for its security and accounting, but also for its husbandry – ie, the maximization of its growth by prudent money management.[2]

The term 'stewardship' connoting the wise use of money and talents was widely accepted within many churches during the 1960s and 1970s – the time when awareness of environmental problems sharply increased. It was probably this availability of the metaphor which first led to its wide application to the natural world. It could easily be extended from money, talents and human resources, to refer to (so-called) natural resources. These also should be used wisely, treated as God's belongings, not ours; they should not be squandered. In other words, by the use of the term 'steward', the natural world is linked to money and resources. Indeed, it would be no exaggeration to say that the financial world is one of the strongest associations behind the concept of stewardship. When humans are described as stewards of the natural world, the language in which this is embedded is usually associated with money. Again and again, the idea of resources, which we must use carefully, look after as if for someone else, encourage to grow, recurs in both Christian and secular writing. The Church of England report, 'Our Responsibility for the Living Environment' (1986), for example, comments:

The Bible pictures mankind in relation to nature as a shepherd, a farm manager, or a household steward – a role which allows us to make use of resources for our needs, but does not permit us to destroy them, since they are entrusted to us for only a limited period.[3]

This idea is seen more strongly in a speech made by Pope John Paul II in August 1985:

Exploitation of the riches of nature must take place according to criteria that take into account not only the immediate needs of people, but also the needs of future generations. In this way the stewardship over nature, entrusted by God to man, will not be guided by short-sightedness or selfish pursuits; rather it will take into account the fact that all created goods are directed to the good of all humanity.[4]

Here the Pope speaks of nature as 'riches' to be 'exploited', but with a view to the future wellbeing of humans. Nature resembles a trust account, which must be allowed to accrue interest for future generations, rather than be selfishly spent in an orgy of present luxury.

Chris Patten MP, in a secular context, is even more explicit. In the interview already cited, he comments: 'I think being prudent about the environment has, frankly, some relationship to being prudent about money.' These are just a few examples of the common link made between stewardship of nature and of money. One could almost compare the natural world to a giant, all-embracing bank account, containing food, clothes, riches, medicines, companions, leisure facilities, landscapes, views and climate regulators! We are here to look after it, cultivate it, develop it, use it – but prudently, as we have it in trust. We must not destroy it by 'spending it all at once'.

This perception of stewardship portrays God as a rich man who has handed his riches over to humanity to use to greatest advantage. Thus humanity is a kind of investor – intended to use the resources to the master's and its own best advantage, to make them grow. The master is thus no longer actively involved with his possessions, although there will ultimately be a reckoning when the steward has to account for the way in which he has used the finances entrusted to him. The primary emphasis is on the steward and the use of the resources, rather than on the relationship between the master and the steward.

However, as I commented earlier, stewardship can be perceived in different ways. Sometimes it is viewed in a more traditional way: the relationship between God and humanity is like that between master and servant on a feudal estate. A steward in this sense would be expected to demonstrate unquestioning obedience to his master due to his lower rank in the social hierarchy, and to demonstrate a probably equal degree of control over those beneath him. His actions could only be questioned by the master. God is the ultimate power and authority; he issues commands, and his will is absolute. The steward, humanity, is in a position of delegated power and responsibility. Here, the focus is very much on the relationship of the master and servant. The possessions of the master, in this case the rest of the natural world, appear to be in a powerless position. Owned by one, and managed by the other, they are at the lowest end of this hierarchy. It seems to me that both of these perceptions of the relationships between God, humanity and the rest of the natural world are deeply flawed, theologically, politically and ecologically.

Stewardship: a theological problem

Both the above perceptions of stewardship have great difficulty in accommodating the idea of God's action or presence in the world. God is understood to be an absentee landlord, who has put humanity in charge of his possessions. In itself, this excludes the presence of God in humanity or in the natural world: it is absurd to speak of a master 'indwelling' his steward, or his possessions. Within the framework of the model, God's action and presence in the world are largely mediated through humans. This is so of both the feudal perception, where God the master leaves man in charge of his estate, and also of the financial perception, where God, the owner of financial resources, puts them in the trust of humanity, the investor, to use for

74

him as best it can. This separation of God from the world was one of the criticisms of Christianity brought by Lynn White Jnr. in his famous article in 1967, 'The Historical Roots of our Ecologic Crisis'.[5] White contests that in destroying native religions, with their beliefs in God or gods dwelling in the world, Christianity desacralised the natural world, and laid it open to exploitation. White's article has frequently been criticized on historical grounds. None the less, it seems likely that a theology which separates God from the natural world is less likely to respect it than one which sees God as indwelling – a pantheistic or panentheistic model.[6]

The problematic nature of this view of the nature of God is increased by the tendency of Christians to accept theological models as absolutes, or the 'way things are'. Once stewardship is believed to constitute the God/humanity/rest of the natural world relationship, holding a different model alongside (such as that of God indwelling the world) becomes difficult. In this respect also, stewardship poses yet another theological problem.

Political implications of stewardship

Although the term 'steward' has now been adopted in the West as a convenient way of expressing man's place in the natural world, its implications are not only ecological. The feudal perception in particular has political consequences since it is based on a power hierarchy of control and obedience. As we have already seen, God is ultimately in control, as a benign dictator. It is against this model of the God/human relationship that many branches of recent theology – liberation theology, feminist theology, process theology – have been reacting. These theologians argue that it is the triumphalist models of God as sovereign and ruler, dominating the world, that help to sustain, if not to create, the oppressive, hierarchical societies in which we live. Feminist theologians reject the stress on the divine as 'masculine', with its accompanying characteristics of control and emotional detachment. Liberation theologians, such as Gustavo Gutierrez and Juan Luis Segundo argue that God suffers, is in solidarity with the poor, liberating them from the oppression in which they live. Moltmann goes so far as to say:

> The one who knows God in the lowliness and weakness of the dying of Christ, does not know him in the dreamed-of exaltation and divinity of the man who seeks God, but in the humanity which he has abandoned, rejected and despised.[7]

'Stewardship' sits very uneasily with these theological standpoints, which both emerge from and address the political and social conditions in which the majority of the world's population are forced to live. 'Stewardship' originates from a human relationship which has now, consciously at least, been condemned: slavery. The political message encoded in stewardship is one of power and oppression; of server and the served. Its popularity in the Western world could be said to reflect the dominant positions which the rich economies have over the struggling nations of the Third World. For those who lead and benefit from these economies, stewardship can be used without mounting a challenge to the status quo.

While to this extent acceptable in the West, at another level, 'stewardship' fails to correspond to political structures which we ourselves advocate. We no longer respect societies based on the model of the benign dictatorship. Political values over an increasing proportion of the earth's surface at least advocate political freedom, democracy, and consultation (even if their actions belie their words). We would not respect someone for unquestioningly obeying the orders of a dictator, however convinced they were that she or he was good, nor would we respect a leader that expected it. Dorothée Soelle makes this point when she says:

> How can we stand a God-talk based on the refusal of democratisation and self-determination? If God is not ready to give up his power, if he does not want us to determine our fate, we cannot trust him. He is then nothing but a somewhat liberal capitalist, and our trust in that end makes us more childish than we are. The God we are in need of is not a private owner, nor a capitalist with a human face. *There is only one legitimation of power, and that is to share it.*[8]

Of course, God is not a political leader in the normal sense (for instance, elections are impossible!) but the language used to speak about him/her is important. If slaves of God, then being slaves of a 'representative on earth' is made more acceptable; if unquestioning obedience to God, then an inability to exercise independence of thought in other matters is made more likely. A model of God which engages with the political concerns with which we are surrounded must resemble democracy rather than dictatorship.[9]

The idea of stewardship originates in a society which is based on slavery or serfdom, and represents a despotic and autocratic form of government, a fact which is particularly clear when considering it in the feudal context. In this respect alone, the term is unsuitable for use in modern society.

The ecological implications of stewardship

Speaking of 'stewardship of the natural world' has important ecological consequences. Certain assumptions seem to lie behind or to be associated with it. Firstly, there is a strong sense of humanity's separation from the rest of the natural world. Following on from this there may be a cluster of other beliefs: that the natural world is a human resource, that humans are really in control of nature, that nature is dependent on humanity for its management.

These are, of course, complex and difficult questions. The question of how far humanity is separated from nature has been asked for thousands of years. In a very obvious, although perhaps underestimated sense, humans are entirely part of, and dependent on, the natural world. Humanity evolved within the natural world. We share part of the genetic codings of all living species, especially other mammals. We are part of the food chain; we eat and are eaten; our bodies are the hosts of bacteria, yeasts, parasites; when we die, our bodies form the parts of other living creatures. We are, as are all living things, dependent on the natural cycles of water, nitrogen, carbon dioxide. If the rains fail, as they frequently do, we starve. Yet, in an equally obvious sense, humans seem to be different from the rest of the natural world. Humans have the most developed cerebral cortex of all animals; they are more intelligent, although not unique in possessing intelligence. This enables a greater control over their environment than any other species; witness the construction of amenities to better the human condition: houses, roads, schools. To this extent, humans exercise a degree of dominance over the natural world unsurpassed by any other species.

It would be foolish to claim that humans are not the dominant species at present existing on this planet. However, this is not evidence that humanity has been in some theological or even philosophical sense 'set apart' as manager or governor, God's representative on earth. Humans have evolved with unique characteristics, as have all species, and this difference has enabled them to move to a position of control. But if, for instance, there was abrupt climatic change, humanity could easily become extinct, whilst other species, better equipped for such an event, could gain the ascendancy. In the light of evolution, the idea of human metaphysical 'set-apartness' becomes impossible to justify. However, the concept of stewardship continues to support this set-apartness.

The other ecological beliefs which cluster around stewardship are of a similar nature. The contention that man is needed to look after the earth stems from a pre-evolutionary understanding of nature. It is perhaps influenced by the idea that nature is 'fallen' and imperfect, requiring human activity to perfect it. In the light of evolutionary science, the idea that earth 'needs to be managed' by humans is obviously a nonsense, although still maintained by some theologians. The earth existed for millions of years without humanity, life flourished, evolution continued. If humanity should become extinct, as all species ultimately seem to do, then life on earth will continue to flourish, as it went on after the dinosaurs and after the dodo. There are parts of the earth where humans have never seriously lingered (although perhaps will do): the heart of Antarctica, the inner rainforests. These are not 'managed' or 'stewarded', and they do not lack anything. Stewardship is inappropriate for some of the planet some of the time, some of it for all of the time (the deep oceans) and all of it for some of the time – that is, before humanity evolved and after its extinction.

The work of the scientist James Lovelock,[10] although by no means unanimously accepted among the scientific establishment, brings a new dimension to this insight. He considers that the planet acts as one huge, self-regulating organism, keeping the atmosphere and temperature of the planet capable of sustaining life. He points out that, for instance, solar energy has increased by 25% in the time that life has existed on the planet, yet the temperature has never increased or fallen by more than five degrees. The crucial regulatory organisms, he argues, are the tropical rainforests and the algae growths of the deep oceans. It is these which act to control the conditions of the planet, and it is these which are most important to the continuance of life on earth. Seen from this perspective, humanity is no manager, nor steward; in fact its position is less central to life than that of many other organisms – which, at present, humans are intent on destroying.

It is this very destruction that brings me to question another, associated belief: that man actually is ultimately in control of the natural world – or, to phrase it another way, that man is *able* to be a steward. To be a successful steward, either in the feudal or the financial sense, it is necessary to understand that which is being controlled. But the natural world is not like an estate, nor like money in this respect. It is composed of complex ecosystems and atmospheric conditions that we do not understand and cannot predict. The depth of uncertainty about global warming is one illustration of this. Scientists are neither sure that it is happening nor sure of what will happen if it is. The immunity developed by so-called pest species to poisons such as DDT is another example; malarial mosquitos cannot be eliminated by this pesticide. The greatest chemists and biologists alive are quick to point out how little we understand of the natural world in which we live. *Can* we then be stewards of the natural world?

Saying this leaves me open to the criticism that I am both asserting human helplessness and simultaneously arguing that humans bear responsibility for the preservation of the natural world; that I am both urging that humans do something, and then claiming that they are unable to do it. This is not my intention at all. I am not, as I have said, suggesting that humans are completely helpless. We may not have the regulatory effect on the world's environment of the deep sea algae, for instance, but we are capable of causing vast environmental devastation (while probably not extinction of life). I am suggesting that our control is only partial and that we must see it in the perspective of the many things we do not know and perhaps will never know. It is surely the case that when humans admit their partial knowledge they will take their responsibilities more, rather than less seriously.

The final belief associated with stewardship of the natural world which I wish to question is perhaps the most pervasive and powerful: that the rest of the natural world is there for us to use. It is our resource. This attitude is implicit in the feudal perception of stewardship, in that the natural world is regarded as an estate, to be treated as the master chooses, but is explicit in the financial model of stewardship, which sees the rest of the natural world as it sees money.

Money is, obviously, a human invention, created by us and for us. It has no function outside human society, and is entirely a human resource. Accumulating more of it, and using it prudently, is one of the aims of Western society at least. But the natural world around us is not a human creation. It does function outside human society. It existed for millions of years before humans evolved, and, as I have said, it will exist after we have become extinct. In this fundamental respect, it is not like money. Yet the language of financial stewardship persists in treating it so.

Everything that lives must use other, living and non-living materials in order to survive. Humans, of course, must do this too. However, the model of stewardship of the natural world contains the implicit idea that *this is what they are there for.* The reason for the existence of minerals in the soil, trees in the forest, fish in the sea, is for the benefit of humanity. Thus Pope John Paul II could say, 'all created goods are directed to the good of humanity.' It is this idea which is the most dangerous assumption contained within the concept of stewardship. Its implications are immense. If the natural world is like a huge bank account which we may use, however prudently, the environmental ethic which flows from this is entirely human-centred. Provided that something can be justified as benefiting humanity, or some of humanity, it is morally acceptable under a stewardship ethic.

There has been little criticism of the implications of this idea of stewardship. However, the environmental philosophers, Richard and Val Routley comment in their essay, *Human Chauvinism and Environmental Ethics*, that stewardship is

> inconsistent with a deeper environmental ethic because it implies policies of complete interference . . . [stewardship] would, in fact, prefer to see the earth's land surfaces reshaped along the lines of the tame and comfortable, but ecologically impoverished European small farm and village landscape . . . man's role, like that of a farm manager, is to make nature productive by his efforts, though not means that will deliberately deplete its resources.[11]

Cultivation of all practicable land for use is reasonable, and even desirable in terms of a stewardship ethic. The destruction of wildwood or wilderness for agriculture to feed an expanding human population would be quite acceptable. The flooding of river valleys, such as the Loire project in France, to produce hydro-electric power could be defended on a stewardship ethic. Indeed, stewardship would not only allow but actually encourage total use or cultivation of the natural world for human benefit. That nature should be productive by our standards is built into the stewardship assumption.

These assumptions, which lie behind most uses of stewardship, demonstrate that stewardship is an anthropocentric ethic, which considers it to be better not only for humans, but for the rest of the natural world, for nature to be managed and made fruitful by human standards.

Stewardship in secular political discourse

Although the concept of stewardship of the natural world originated in religious discourse, it has since been abstracted into international political discussion, usually losing its ultimate religious referent, God. This is not always the case. Margaret Thatcher commented in a speech to the United Nations made in 1989, 'We are the Lord's creatures, the trustees of life on this planet, charged with preserving life itself.' Although the word 'steward' is not used, 'trustee' has here a similar ring – a divine charge to preserve, to look after the planet. It has not yet been extracted from a religious context. However, in most political language, 'steward' is used without reference to God. This goes on to pose problems of interpretation, since steward, by its very nature implies that someone else's possessions or property is being looked after. Yet if not for God, for whom could we be stewards? This question is addressed rather flippantly by the naturalist Richard Mabey:

> On whose behalf are we stewards of the planet? Not, presumably, its literal owners. God then, or Gaia? I suspect that most of us who use the word might answer 'the planet itself' which is, at best, a piece of sophistry and at worst, a reworking of the patronising view that nature needs to be in human custody for its own good. This is asking for a warder, not a steward.[12]

He does, however, raise an important question – is non-theistic stewardship exercised on behalf of the planet? For future generations? Or is there no particular referent at all? It has been used in all three senses, but all have problems. If humanity is the steward for the planet, or Gaia, as Mabey says, this carries the suggestions that the earth has a will, or can give commands, or has preferences as to how it develops; that the earth needs humans to manage it, and,

83

from this, that humans are separated from it. All of these are open to question.

There are fewer obvious difficulties in envisaging humanity as the steward of the earth on behalf of future generations, as encapsulated in the environmentalist phrase, 'we do not inherit the earth from our ancestors, we borrow it from our children'. It has the advantage that unlike Gaia, future generations will possess wills and preferences. However, as with all models of stewardship, humanity is still separated from the rest of the natural world, and the implication still is that it needs to be managed. Further, it suggests that future generations actually own the natural world.

Having said this, stewardship often seems to be used in political discourse without anything corresponding to a 'master.' This can mean either or both of two things. 'Steward' may become a vague term, with no real meaning, but suggesting the idea of responsible use, or 'steward' and 'master' may become telescoped into one, and when spoken of, stewardship actually means a form of mastery, in that we decide when the rest of the natural world should be used, and for what.

Stewardship of the natural world, whether Christian or otherwise, then, remains profoundly anthropocentric and unecological, legitimating and encouraging increased human use of the natural world.

In conclusion

I suggested at the beginning of this chapter that the idea of stewardship can act as a comfortable concept blinkering us to the deeper philosophical and theological problems raised by the environmental crisis. Stewardship allows humanity to continue with exploitative attitudes towards the natural world, often with the justification that God has given this authority. It certainly softens existing attitudes of domination and triumphalism towards the rest of the natural world, by adding an element of responsibility. However, it fails to change the fundamental human-centredness of the original premise. It is this concept of stewardship which allows Chris Patten MP to accept the building of a theme park on Rainham Marshes and a marina in Cardiff Bay, both wildlife reserves, in order to serve human recreational and aesthetic ends. It allows the Church of England to make the statement advocating stewardship quoted earlier, in order to avoid passing legislation to ban intensive farming and fox hunting on church-owned land. Perhaps James Lovelock is right to comment:

> From a Gaian viewpoint, all attempts to rationalise [domination of the planet] with man in charge are as doomed to failure as the similar concept of benevolent colonialism. They all assume man is the possessor of this planet; if not the owner then the tenant . . . All human societies in one way or another regard the world as their farm.[13]

Notes

1. Interview in *The Guardian*, 5 February 1990.
2. *The Masonic Tract on Charity Matters* (Lewis Masonic, 1979).
3. Report of the General Synod Board for Social Responsibility, 'Our Responsibility for the Living Environment' (Church House Publishing 1986).
4. Pope John Paul II, speech at the United Nations Centre for the Environment in Nairobi, August 1985, quoted in Sean McDonagh, *The Greening of the Church* (Chapman 1990), p. 181.
5. Lynn White Jnr., 'The Historical Roots of our Ecologic Crisis', *Science* 155, 10 March 1967.
6. Although there are also problems with pantheistic and panentheistic views, in that the natural world is revered for the spirit it contains, rather than for itself.

7. Jürgen Moltmann, *The Crucified God* (SCM Press 1985).
8. Dorothée Soelle, *Beyond Mere Dialogue: on being Christian and Socialist* (Detroit, Mich. 1978).
9. A thorough and careful consideration of the relations between models of God and political models of the state may be found in David Nicholls, *Deity and Domination* (Routledge 1989).
10. James Lovelock, *Gaia: A New Look at Life on Earth* (Oxford University Press 1979, 1987).
11. Reprinted in *Environmental Philosophy*, ed. John Mannison, Michael McRobbie and Richard Routley. (Monograph Series No. 2, Australia University National Press 1980).
12. Richard Mabey, 'Woodman Woodman, Spare those Trees', *The Guardian* 7 July 1990.
13. Lovelock, p. 145.

4

An Ecological Spirituality:
Insights from Teilhard de Chardin

IAN CARTER

The threat posed by pollution and exploitation of the world's natural resources is one of the most serious facing us today. Many solutions are proposed to this evil, but often there is little serious analysis of the solutions offered; any response is better than sitting back and doing nothing, it seems.

This contribution looks at the writings of a French Jesuit priest and scientist, Pierre Teilhard de Chardin, mainly written between 1920 and 1950, to see what insights we can gain there. His writing was done before the world became conscious of green concerns (the publication of Rachel Carson's *Silent Spring* in 1962 may be seen as a significant rallying point). His writing remained unpublished in his lifetime because his views offended his superiors in the Jesuit order. This meant he was largely denied the refinement of critical help from his contemporaries. In his writings he presents himself as one with an understanding and love of science as well as a deep spirituality.

Teilhard was a pioneer. He was steeped in modern science and especially ideas about evolution. This was very much a part of his vision. But he could not just leave his ideas about evolution in the past. They had to look forward to the future as well. He was not just interested in God as the watchmaker who 'did create' everything, but as a continuing agent of progress into the future. The direction of this future progress was a special concern to him. He saw progress coming through people and through changes in the way people relate to each other, especially in their thinking.

He was aware of disturbing realities in the world. He was especially conscious of the destructive powers of people in two world wars, having himself served on the front lines of the French army for four and a half years in World War One. Despite the mindless slaughter and the shattering cruelty of that war, he kept a conviction of the mysterious purpose that there is for things.

There are indications of a similar attitude to ecological problems. In 1924 he wrote, 'The easily won novelties of the earth will be exhausted. Men will then become more distinctly aware of the essential need of knowledge if they are to have fuller being; they will find themselves faced with vaster and more urgent problems, expressed in clearer terms.'[1] Even then he could predict the result of exploitation without moral reflection. In 1947 he wrote in a similar vein: 'In recent years voices of alarm have been raised periodically in many quarters pointing to the fast-growing gulf between technical and moral progress in the world today. The perils of this situation are plain to anyone.'[2]

The crisis is complex. Progress brings provision of food, health, education, prosperity for a growing world population. Many believe that the cost to our shrinking resources and worsening environment requires deeper issues to be faced. Hard decisions have to be made in a situation where it seems we cannot live in the present without affecting the future. A lot of Teilhard's writings concern his prediction of what the future holds – the way people react in response to God and their consciousness of their special role in creation.

He was aware of a progress in evolution, and he believed he could see signs of where this progress could lead in the future. He thought the next step forward in evolution would be in human thought. As human thought becomes more aware of itself, Teilhard saw signs of it organising itself collectively. He thought the result of this organisation would be evolution into a new thinking order. This order would have the ability to solve any purely technical problem.

He argued that the human impetus for research, the human faith in life and progress, the human belief in the collective abilities of people, would be used to promote growth in 'complexity and consciousness'. In this way progress in the technical sphere would always be matched by progress in the moral and spiritual sphere; thus there need be no fear of exploitation or oppression.

Teilhard was conscious of the way research is becoming increasingly organised and directable. As a research scientist himself he knew at first hand the thrill of a new discovery, the awakening of an idea that can provide a key to the solution of a long-standing problem. He knew the need to work in teams, to direct the efforts of many different specialists to an agreed end in order to achieve the goal. This he saw as no luxury, but a necessary function of modern life.

Teilhard would have had few surprises with the achievements of technology in the second half of this century. Indeed he welcomed the development of nuclear capability. He argued that this process is one which must continue if we are to achieve our purpose. He suggested that the right way forward in the present crisis is to direct whole research teams to find the solutions: 'Since its birth science has made its greatest advances when stimulated by some particular problem of life needing a solution.'[3]

Because he is convinced of progress, he is always sure that a solution can be found. This assumption may amount to his putting his trust in the power of the human mind to procure what it wants, or it may be a deep spiritual insight: we will look further at this in the next section.

Teilhard was not just a scientist with a Christian faith. He was an exemplary priest with a missionary vocation. His thought was fundamentally theological in scope. As a man of faith he could see that what needs to be coupled to science is an attitude that puts Christ at the centre and is aware of the holism of the universe. His ideas about evolution could not leave his beliefs about God untouched. He could not believe that God is a scientifically superfluous hypothesis any more than he believed reason and empirical method to be irrelevant to theology. He thought that what we do helps to build the fulfilment of our spiritual as well as our material hopes. Indeed they can bring to Christ a little fulfilment by our service of him. Teilhard saw in this possibility a unitary design. He suggested that Christ could be found at the centre of all and was there as a purpose for action.

Teilhard had an intense religious as well as scientific zeal. In his writings he confronts boldly those who become schizophrenic in their religious activities, separating them off from life, and those who see human activity as an end in itself which is self-justifying. This chapter seeks to look at the insights Teilhard gives in his sacramental approach to nature and looks at the way he urges people to be conscious of the larger dimension of their efforts.

A sacramental approach to nature

Within the biblical perspective it is clear that the human creature occupies a place of central significance in the created order. When God said in Genesis 1.8 that man had 'dominion' over creation, this is sometimes taken as an axiom that nature has no purpose but to serve people.

One of the ways Christianity has been blamed for the

environmental disaster we are facing is the doctrine of human dominion over the rest of creation.[4] However, whether alternative approaches based on romantic notions of archaic peoples who lived 'in harmony with nature' are any more plausible has yet to be proven. The doctrine of human domination is thankfully not the only way in which Christians have approached creation, nor does it necessarily imply absolute rights to destroy. An alternative approach is espoused by the Orthodox Church which has always had a profoundly sacramental view of nature, and Teilhard is an example of the Western theologians who have expressed a remarkable understanding of Christ's continuous and dynamic presence in the world.

At the very least Christians, like their creator, should look at creation and see its goodness. Like their creator they should be capable of exercising creative care to see it achieves its proper end. Some Christians have gone further and seen in the 'open book' of creation not just signs of the creator's action, but the creator incarnate in the world. Teilhard puts himself in this group. He believed Christ was in every particle of creation.

We see this especially in a passage written in Jersey in 1919 where his conversation with matter ran,

> Blessed be you mighty matter . . . you who resist us and yield to us . . . the sap of our souls, the hand of God, the flesh of Christ: it is you, matter, I bless . . . I acclaim you as the divine milieu charged with creative power, as the ocean charged with the spirit, as the clay moulded and infused with life by the incarnate world.[5]

Some Christian teaching imagines a creator God who at the beginning set the universe in motion and has left it to run itself since. No so here. God is very much involved in creation, immanent in the world. Wherever we look, God is. Teilhard believes there can be no radical separation of creator from creation. God is involved in all the change, through and through. He is the changer, the change and the one who is changed.

One way in which Teilhard expresses this is by using the term 'the Cosmic Christ'. This is Christ who is found in every atom and molecule of existence. Much more than looking at the 'book of nature' and finding God revealed in its structure and symmetry, he believes that we find evidence of him physically and literally all around us, if we are willing to look:

> All around us Christ is physically active in order to control all things . . . he ceaselessly animates, without disturbing, all the earth's processes. And in return Christ gains physically from every one of them. Everything that is good in the Universe (that is everything that goes towards unification through effort) is gathered up by the incarnate word as a nourishment that it assimilates, transforms and divinises.[6]

The reality of his belief in this presence is emphasised in this passage and others by the repetition of the word 'physically'. However, by itself this belief does not get us anywhere. According to this view, Christ may be just as much present in the plastics of the refuse tip as in the trees of the rain forest, in nuclear waste as in peat bog. Respecting matter as created material gets us nowhere in ecological terms – trees and acid rain, ozone and CFCs all have material components.

The passage also shows another theme of Teilhard's thought – that of a goal, of a direction to evolution. His idea of a convergence upon Christ is central to Teilhard's understanding of the last things, and he talks of Christ-Omega, a unifying principle within creation. Perhaps his Catholic belief in transubstantiation was of significance in his approach to Christ's indwelling of matter which is presented to us in a particularly all-encompassing way. In this presentation, Christ is almost like the ultimate 'black hole' that will suck everything in, bending space into a vortex that converges on him, pulling everything towards himself.

However, if we analyse what is converging to the centre in this system, it is human thought – consciousness. As matter becomes ever more complex, so 'consciousness' or 'spirit' converges in. Because of this the place of mankind is central to Teilhard's thinking, and so must inevitably colour any conclusions he draws in ecological thinking.

Indeed in Teilhard's system this progress in the 'cerebralisation' of mankind is the only place where evolution is now continuing. So the place of humanity in this system is emphasised again and again. Indeed just as Teilhard uses the word 'biosphere' for the natural world he coined the word 'noosphere' for the envelope of consciousness above the biosphere; and he projects a hierarchy, a superiority onto this noosphere.

There are of course many modern approaches that invite us to embark upon a creation-centred spirituality, not the least of which is that described by Matthew Fox (in, for example, *Original Blessing: A Primer in Creation Spirituality*, Santa Fe, NM, Bear & Co. Inc., 1983). If we look at these creation-centred spiritualities we often find there is a concentration on the word through whom all things were made, and without whom nothing was made that was made (John's gospel), and a neglect of the word of life who is the atoning sacrifice for our sins, and not only for our sins but for the sins of the whole world (John's epistle). The God presented in creation spiritualities is often very different from the traditional belief about God in orthodox teaching, and especially is often lacking in its understanding of the place and meaning of the cross.

Teilhard's language is always centred on Christ. Teilhard always has a Christology in view. So we might look to him to find both the creation theme and the redemption theme. We find that the significance of both is presented as much bigger and more universal than many traditional statements may allow. He sees the gospel in cosmic terms. Teilhard talks of the resurrection in the same terms as he talks of the last things – it is part of a cosmic awakening, a taking on of a cosmic destiny. Many see this as a distortion rather than an interpretation. It is hardly surprising that his writings were refused publication. To understand what is at issue here, perhaps we should look at the biblical concept of time.

The Bible speaks of time in two ways. It uses the Greek word *chronos* to mean 'space or duration of time'. This word is comparatively rare. Much more frequent is the word *kairos* meaning 'decisive point in time'. Christian teaching often centres on two such decisive points: the *kerygma*, the coming of the good news, and the future of the *parousia*, the fulfilment of the good news. Even for the individual believer, faith can be focused on decisive points in a person's life – conversion, or ultimate hope, for example. For science on the other hand, time is a medium within which observations may be measured and theories proposed. The future will, sometime or other, become the past in an irreversible action. The future offers a reason for development and planning, for prediction and programmes, but not for enduring hope.

Traditional statements of the Christian message often seem to place hope in some far off future that is unattainable in this life. Teilhard is compelled to present a model which is scientific as well as having elements of the traditional. His model of time is an axis with Christ at its origin in creation, Christ in its centre in the incarnation, and Christ at its fulfilment at the *parousia*. His picture of Christ is very much of a force that draws us on, that attracts us from in front.

The historical Christ appeared on earth at a particular time and date. The Christian message relates how that event radiates in time and space and takes shape as a landmark at the crossroads of mankind. From our individual perspective this universal influence can be more important than its location in date and place. We recognise the existence of sorrow, pain and evil in the world, but we also recognise Christ's ultimate victory over all three.

In Teilhard the universal influence is emphasised almost to the exclusion of its historical location. His system has flaws because of his insistence on progress. For example, he cannot cope with evil because of his desire for harmony. Indeed he is so full of hope for the future that in his system no true concept of evil can be allowed to mar our progress towards Christ. In the expectation of inevitable progress no real redemption is necessary.

Issues like the destruction of the rain forest or the ozone layer were not current at the time. Even if they had been it is likely that the evils of such changes would be thought unimportant by Teilhard in terms of the total progress of mankind. They may represent a sin of which we have to repent, a global disaster that has to be transfigured – but the expectation of inevitable progress we find in Teilhard involves a belief that such things will all be transformed into some better plan for nature. Teilhard was aware of the way evolution works, through nature 'red in tooth and claw'. He saw this as a necessary part of progress. Although this may be unfortunate for many individuals, what had ultimate significance for him was the overall progress towards unification. There is here a scientific pragmatism that refuses to judge that there are any costs too high to pay for progress.

A curious coincidence for one who had so much regard for the cosmic significance is that he always hoped he would die on Easter day. This was granted him in 1955. In his writing it is not, however, the individual but the universal significance we find written large and bold. In many passages we can almost hear Teilhard holding a conversation between dogma and his experience of the world. An intuition that strikes Teilhard is that the universe is organised along an axis of time. But this axis is not neutral. It is polarised, orientated – it converges upon Christ, and Christ is the axis along which it runs. Teilhard is making a valiant attempt to reconcile the insights of his religious tradition and his scientific training. One of the difficulties this picture presents to us is the central place it gives to mankind. Because of the superiority he gives to reflection, the medium he is interested in is human thought.

The picture he emphasises is of the numinous dimension of life present in matter itself. He believes matter is not inert, but shows us God, for God fills it through and through: there is an essential link, a unity in him. For Teilhard as for many other authors, acknowledgement of this basic unity in Christ must alter the way we approach creation. They say a vision of the universe in this perspective demands a reverence for the natural world that a vision based on scientific or religious domination over matter can never provide. If matter is seen as dead, inert and radically inferior to the human it is exploitable. But matter which shows us God, which is God, must have important implications for spirituality and may help us in a search for ecologically relevant ideas. However as matter is just as easily represented by pesticides or industrial effluent as living forests, we need to add to this picture some way of choosing why we should respect one rather than the other.

Humanity's approach to nature

If Christians are to have a positive and constructive dialogue with the green movement, and with all who are concerned about the future of our planet, then we need to convert insights into action. So often our statements are seen as irrelevant because they do not result in action which corresponds to the truths they proclaim. Our insights can be negated by a lack of supporting action. The church is happy to use its insights in public worship and private prayer, but hesitates from engaging in political action to change ecologically exploitative structures. There is no serious challenge to our anthropocentric, consumer-led belief in consumption. As we increasingly find ourselves living in the debris of an industrial wonder-world and within a system that values creation and everything in it according to market forces, so we smother ourselves with the sheer volume of our waste.

One of the attitudes that influence this belief is the understanding of the earth as a human resource, as something to be cultivated, as something from which secrets and energies can be won. Progress can often be discerned as an increase in knowledge and power. In Teilhard's system this conquest of nature is seen as fulfilling the purpose of nature which emphasises this attitude. Of course many atheistic authors argue this as well. Where this is presented as the revelation of God's action, it is little wonder that we come into conflict with green concerns. For those who believe God pervades our universe through and through, purpose and value are profoundly connected to him.

Teilhard challenges us to look at the future, to believe in progress, and to co-operate with God in working towards it. We are challenged not just to expand our spirituality so as to see it as more than an other-worldly goal or as a series of ritual acts which put us right with God. We are challenged to channel our energies and to live with an explicit consciousness of a universe which is Christ's body.

'Every process of material growth in the universe is directed towards spirit, and every process of spiritual growth towards Christ. If this hope is justified, the

Christian must be active, and busily active, working as earnestly as the most convinced of those who work to build up the earth, that Christ may continually be born more fully in the world about him.'[7] Teilhard holds out to us a vision in which we work for God by everything we do in the world. Every action in every sphere can be of ultimate significance.

He was determined that his readers should move from a perspective which separates spirit and matter in a false dichotomy, to one which sees their destinies intertwined in evolution; from one which sees the logos as a divine interferer from without, to one which discovers the logos as an inner ordering at the heart of all matter.

There is much in modern psychology that helps our awareness at this point. Many people try to separate radically the forces of good and evil in a false way. They project upon evil all the nasty things within themselves that they don't like. A false polarisation and separation sets in and becomes paranoia – they are good and everything outside is bad. The spiritual goal becomes a quest for an other-worldly perfection, leading back into the individual because that is where it comes from.

This false polarisation can easily affect those involved in green issues. Technology can be seen as an evil which is responsible for all the bad in the environment. This can disguise the problem of an anthropocentric vision that inevitably leads us to rape and squander resources from basic selfish motives. The opposite is presented here. Technology is seen as a good and so there can be no questioning of it.

God challenges us to integrate our personalities, to accept ourselves, the uncomfortable as well as the comfortable emotions, to get rid of our illusory and distorted pictures of ourselves and to participate in the fulness of what we are. Our spiritual goal is a quest to participate as adults in a conversation with others and with God. We can co-operate with others to help them reach their fulfilment as we reach ours. We learn to grow up from a childish ego-centricity to an adult Christo-centricity. We learn to care for and sustain relationships. Teilhard believed that faith can generate the will for such change and that everything needs to be integrated into the task of growth towards cosmic consciousness.

In terms of human action, Teilhard was concerned to activate a zest for life and a will to participate in evolution. He believed human action assisted the evolutionary advance and could apply in any field – business, education, law, science, art, industry. He deduced from his Christology that there was an impetus which drives them along and which they needed to be caught up in if they were to achieve their potential. We need to get caught up in this ardour if we are to play our part in the creativity of God.

In earlier periods it may have been possible to see in the Universe a Great or Cosmic Person controlling mankind and the rest of creation. We now see that at least on the surface of this planet we have a great deal of choice about what is allowed to happen within a system that shows regular and predictable results of actions. Because of this, most reject a traditional understanding of a deity at whose whim the very elements change, and some go so far as to exclude God from their system entirely. However Teilhard had a clear vision of God's numinous presence within nature, and for him this had the potential of dynamizing human activity. He wished to communicate that to others.

The emphasis in Teilhard upon integration, unification and a sense of purpose enabled him to see in our capacity to take charge of what is happening on earth not only the instrument but the living extension of the convergence and unification of mankind with itself and with God. It is unfortunate that because of his emphasis on the superiority of human thought in this process this is of little help in our search for ecological ideals.

A living spirituality

We have seen that Teilhard's sacramental approach to nature tries to present a respect and reverence for creation and to approach a synthesis with his scientific training. Teilhard worked tirelessly to present his picture of reality as a motivation for people to act for the future good of humanity and in the direction he saw as the natural progress of evolution. His christological perspective attempts to show a unity in Christ with the whole of creation.

In Teilhard's day, no doubt, the attempt to find a universal discourse that could encompass both science and Christianity might have seemed possible. However we now recognize that science is not an abstraction – not only must the observer necessarily change the system he is observing by his measurement, but more importantly science is mediated through human institutions. Science also has its own ideologies, its own values emerging from human aspirations for prediction and control. It may be that these ideologies would conflict with those we feel are appropriate in the religious sphere.

The Christian spiritual search leads us to look for meaning and significance by contemplation and reflection on the totality of human experiences and the Christian message. This leads us to change our behaviour, our manner of life and our attitude to other people. This can be done publicly or privately, through liturgy, art, music, words or silence. Our movement in this search can be measured by the way it helps us to improve the quality of our own life and the quality of the lives of those around us as we reflect, re-evaluate, reinterpret. Some perspectives can be limiting, punishing, distorted, others lead us to openness, freedom, harmony.

As we look at life, as we enter into conversation with creation and with God, so we are there with minds formed from our own individual history. We look for resonances or discords with our experience to test out both ourselves and our partner. The conversation begins. We try to interpret and try to understand our meaning within the totality of creation. We bring our questions and try to enter the questions posed by life and God. As the conversation goes on, so the interpretations and questions become common ones. As the conversation goes on, so it becomes more honest.

The thing I most admire in Teilhard is the way that he integrated his interpretive method both of the world and of the Christian message. He found what for him was a possible way-of-being-in-the-world that enabled him to have and to communicate hope and solidarity of will, and which above all took him from thinking about his own humanity to thinking about the necessary community of mankind.

It is difficult for us in the 1990s to look at Teilhard's writings without thinking that they have a naively optimistic belief in progress. Recent wars and other horrors have shown that even the most 'advanced' of cultures are capable of depths of destructive evil as profound as any in history. Even the accumulation of scientific knowledge, of technological capacity and of social organisation seems not to have eradicated evil and suffering in the world, but rather to have disclosed that the good of a few invariably leads to the misery of many. There is no evidence, at least in the short term, of the convergence he speaks of.

There are too many occasions when Christianity is willing to accept the priority of scientific discourse over religious discourse. One result of the long conflict between positivistic scientific philosophy and the church is that many Christians are no longer willing to openly criticize the concealed ideologies of science for fear of further losses. However it is necessary that as Christians who wish to emulate the one who 'humbled himself, taking the form of a servant', we should be ready to criticize a system which

101

presents a moral superiority to the process of prediction and control and expects all other systems to submit to the criticism of this process. There must be a place for an acceptance of evil and imperfection as more than just a lack of data. The presentation of any one model as absolute is bound to cause distortions – especially if it is applied outside its appropriate social institution.

It may be that the main value in this present study is the way it highlights the need for Christians not just to see God and his actions in nature, but to find some way of giving value to particular forms in which we find God in nature. The criteria we use to do this will probably not be found in the scientific approach. A positivistic scientific approach now forms one of the main criteria for public knowledge; but that does not mean that it is necessarily appropriate in all situations or that we must adopt it as the only criterion for truth in Christianity.

Perhaps it is in the interpretative process that new spaces for discussion and conversation need to be created. God is the one to provide us with possibilities, he is the agent of change and leads us into exploration of the new life. There is in Teilhard a mystical passion for sharing the creative action which God calls us to, a witness to meaning for human existence and action, a pointing to the future in God. All these are passions which may usefully direct us to matters of ecological concern. However, we need to find fresh ways of expressing and interpreting them.

We are called to find afresh in our day that space which can transform values in the struggle against anthropo-centrism and dogmatism within the sciences and the church, and to give a commitment to engage in the struggle against economic exploitation and environmental pollution. That struggle may call us to expose false concealed ideologies as well as to submit our own thinking to critical re-evaluation. I pray we have the strength to follow wherever God leads.

Notes

1. *Science and Christ* (Collins 1968), p. 83.
2. *The Future of Man* (Fontana 1969), p. 211.
3. *Phenomenon of Man* (Fontana 1970), p. 274.
4. See Lynn White Jnr., 'The Historical Roots of our Ecologic Crisis', *Science*, vol. 155, 1967, pp. 1203–7.
5. *Hymn of the Universe* (Fount 1977), p. 64.
6. *Science and Christ*, p. 59.
7. *Science and Christ*, p. 68.

5

Why Matthew Fox Fails to Change the World

MARGARET GOODALL and JOHN READER

Reading Matthew Fox is like consuming large amounts of strawberry jelly. It slips down very easily, giving an initial impression of something pleasant, but, in the longer term, it offers little of real substance or sustenance.

Fox's writing is similar to his lectures, a bold array of glittering theological sparklers, culled almost at random from previous displays, combined with a number of highly attractive but contentious contemporary ideas to form a vivid but fleeting image of harmony and well-being.[1] For a moment there is light and anticipation, but then the darkness returns. Perhaps this is yet another form of consumer religion emanating from the United States, offering instant reconciliation with God, the cosmos and anything else there might happen to be out there. This is cheap grace, convenient and neatly packaged but somewhat lacking in depth and integrity.

Does this really matter? There are those who believe it does, but they may be in danger of attributing a seriousness and a credibility to the work that it cannot possibly warrant. Maybe Fox's most ardent opponents are, in fact, competing for the same market. Our grace is a bit more expensive, it will cost you a confession or two, but it will last you longer. Which then is the better product? If this is all that there is, what is there to choose between the two?

There are a couple of interesting issues here, one less important, one more so. First, the less important. Fox's opponents appear to be making an unsupported assumption about the man's popularity. They take the fact that his books are selling well and that his lecture tours are well subscribed to mean that everybody who reads or listens to him is automatically a convert. Fortunately, this is not true. Many are curious about what Fox is saying but many are dubious as well. His work has been well received by some in the churches who are concerned with matters ecological, but there are far more who have never even heard of him, nor are ever likely to. Of those who are, some at least are quite capable of seeing through the glitzy facade and wheeling out the traditional theological criticisms. Academic theology has not taken him seriously enough as yet to launch its deconstruction job. He may not be worth taking seriously. The man is an entertainer, not a serious theologian.

The second issue is deeply important, at least to theologians, but one that very few have yet taken seriously enough. What if we are *all* entertainers, in that sense, offering a variety of religious products to a shrinking and largely uninterested market? If there are no absolutes any longer, no universal truths, no guaranteed paths to salvation, what is there to choose between one product and another? After all, do we not create our own God or gods in order to meet our particular needs, fashion them in our own image and then wrap them up in the language of Truth or Value in order to make them worth believing in? As Don Cupitt says, there is no God 'out there', only the yearning and longing within ourselves for something that must be better than we are.[2] If this is the way things are then what makes one god better than any other?

The conflict in the Gulf was a classic example of this. Both sides claimed that 'God' was on their side. Of course they did: that is one of the functions that the word has always fulfilled. 'God' legitimates what you want to do. 'God' makes it OK to bomb the hell out of each other, whichever side you are on. If you cannot invoke God then resort to other excuses, like the struggle for a new world order. It does not matter what words you use, we know what you are doing. Of course each side criticizes the other for making the same claims about God; they cannot both be right. Yet they are both right if it is legitimate to use the word 'God' in that way, and they are both wrong if it is not.

How then is it possible to say that it is wrong to use the word God in a particular way? The most that could be said may be that different people use the word differently. I may use it to refer to a benign father figure who acts as the voice of conscience; you may use it to refer to a life force which is at the heart of creation. It is possible for the guardians of any tradition, priests or theologians, to say that there are boundaries for the use of the word within that particular tradition. Their task, then, is to set the limits of meaning of the technical terms of their tradition. They are the keepers of the word, in charge of official interpretation. This is not to say that the ordinary religious believer either shares or understands those interpretations, but, for the sake of the survival of the institution there needs to be somebody who can say either that you are no longer part of the club, or that what you are talking about is not God. All theological or religious statements should be prefaced with, 'In my tradition we use the word God/salvation or whatever to mean . . .'. In another tradition it may be used in another way.

On what basis, then, can we criticize Matthew Fox? If he is claiming to be part of and an interpreter of the Christian tradition, then he can be criticized for going beyond the bounds of what is acceptable within that. The problem with that is that there is no consensus on what those bounds are. Is he still talking about the Christian God, for instance? Some are obviously happy that he is, some are less convinced, and this is not surprising when it seems that we do not know what we are talking about in the first place. Is he perhaps offering an illegitimate interpretation of some of the tradition's sources? Again, it is certainly possible to argue that his use of the writings of people like Meister Eckhart and Julian of Norwich is somewhat dubious. He is certainly very selective in his choice of material and one-sided in his interpretation of those less amenable to his arguments. However, he has a point to make, and a perfect right to interpret as he wants; indeed, one might say that new ideas or paradigm shifts only occur through outrageous and innovative interpretations. Perhaps he is pushing back the boundaries of what are acceptable interpretations within the tradition. It has been said that Fox is a direct link into definitely anti-Christian thought, for instance, New Age ideas or spiritualism. Well, there again, who is to say that these are automatically beyond the pale?

We do want to criticize Fox, but on other grounds. We suggest that what he writes is sloppy romantic rubbish which appeals to a certain type of believer, notably the affluent type who is largely shielded from political reality. In other words, Fox's work is going to fail in its own terms because it will have a negligible impact upon those who make the vital decisions which affect the future of the environment.

The first question that we need to ask about any religious language is, 'How is it being used?' or possibly, 'What function is it playing in the lives of those who are using it?' It seems that there are three basic answers to such questions. Religious language can be employed as a form of legitimation, rubber-stamping either the status quo or

107

some other approach which someone wants to adopt instead. This is what happens in the 'God is on our side' statements in the context of conflict. Second, it can be used as an integrating factor, offering people a sense of belonging to a community or a tradition. Third, it can provide a basis for the critique of current attitudes and practice, suggesting that something better is both possible and desirable. Often we use it in a mixture of all three without being fully aware that that is what we are doing. We would like to advocate placing the emphasis upon the critical function of religious language. We recognize that the other functions are around as well, particularly the integrating one, but want essentially to employ the terminology of the Christian tradition in order to provide the motivation to strive for ways of living that are preferable to what we have at the moment. If others want to do something different, that is fine, because we recognize that religious language can be used in other ways.

With that in mind, we would want to say that Fox's work is essentially legitimating. It may not support the status quo exactly, but what it does seem to support is one of the latest American alternative lifestyles, living 'green', if you like. His is an attempt to provide legitimation for this from within the Christian tradition, hence his constant use of traditional sources, which otherwise would be irrelevant. It leads him to play fast and loose with certain elements of the tradition, and this annoys establishment theologians. We are less bothered about that than about the fact that it does not seem that Fox's contribution gets us very far politically. Nevertheless, Fox does attempt to link his work in with liberation theology, much in the same way as he attempts to link it with any other fashionable theological approach. This is not convincing, simply because it is far too superficial and fails to acknowledge the possible conflicts between concern for human beings and concern for the natural world. The political objectives of the two movements may well come into conflict in specific instances when choices have to be made and priorities set. Which will be of more value, human life or the rest of creation? Reading Fox one would suspect that it would be the former, in which case it is difficult to say that he is actually proposing a consistent ecological ethic.

He displays a similar superficiality in his use of scientific discourse when he suggests that it is possible to establish a new mysticism by combining science and cosmology. It is as if he wants to take scientific language as being literally true, and then appropriate it to his own theology. We cannot see many scientists, even those sympathetic to religion, being prepared to adopt such a simplistic approach. But this is characteristic of the way that Fox works: he takes what suits him from whatever source seems fashionable and mixes it all up to produce his own personal cocktail. The end product is tasty and entertaining but ultimately unsatisfying. His work is a warning against the dangers of consumer religion. It will not do in the end to make out of religion anything that you want; there must be some boundaries and guidelines, even if they are not the ones that the theologians normally imagine. Being faithful to tradition or to sources is perhaps less vital than offering an interpretation which stimulates both critical thought and action. Fox's work is much too cosy and comfortable to provoke any real challenge to current attitudes and practice.

A useful way of assessing Fox's work is to identify the presence of what could be called ideological content. We will follow here the suggestions of John B. Thompson in his recent book on ideology and the media.[3] Thompson defines ideology as any use of language which serves to conceal relations of domination. He then presents five categories to aid the recognition of such relations. It is important to note that he says that the fact that such categories may be found does not in itself mean that we are encountering the ideological use of language, nor that these are the only possible forms that ideology can take. However, we think it is safe to assume that, if these particular forms do turn up consistently in the work of a specific author, then there are good grounds for at least having doubts and suspicions about its nature and intent.

We shall now describe Thompson's five categories. The first is 'legitimation' and covers attempts to show that a line of thought or action is worthy of support. Such appeals to legitimacy can be made in a number of ways. Rational argument may be used, but so may reference to either the sanctity of tradition or to the personal authority or charisma of an individual. One form in which this might be expressed is by describing arrangements which serve only the interests of a minority as if they served the interests of everybody. Another alternative is to treat the present as if it is a straightforward continuation of a long-standing tradition.

Clearly, such approaches are more than familiar to students of religion. Recourse to tradition is a well-established means of legitimation and, as Thompson says, is not necessarily ideological. However, as those of us who have attended Fox's lectures know, his idiosyncratic use of tradition is combined with a heavy emphasis upon his own personality. This may make us wary of much that he wishes to communicate.

The second category Thompson calls 'dissimulation', meaning instances where relations of domination are concealed or obscured by the manipulation of language. Again, this can happen in a number of ways. Terms may be switched without explanation or justification from one subject to another: actions or institutions may be re-described in a form which suggests a positive evaluation. Euphemisms can be used as a deliberate attempt to shift meaning, eg calling a concentration camp a rehabilitation

110

centre. As we shall see, Fox is a master at redefining the meaning of words and at applying terms to an unfamiliar context in a way that suits his own interpretations.

A third ideological use of language is 'unification'. This is when individuals or groups are lumped together under one heading, thus negating or denying their divisions and differences. Fox's attempts to appropriate various strands of the Christian mystical tradition plus his superficial linkage with liberation theology, both seem to be examples of this approach. Such claims need to be examined with great care.

The fourth category reverses this, instead splitting up artificially opponents who might be capable of mounting an effective corporate challenge to the proposed interpretation. Distinctions and differences are over-emphasized and there are also moves to create an Enemy, the Other out there, who then becomes the object of revulsion. Once more, Fox appears to be dangerously close to this, particularly in his categorizing of 'goodies' and 'baddies' within the Christian tradition. It is surely this tendency which gives rise to the fears of a possible alliance in his thought with anti-semitism and its blatant scapegoating.

Finally, Thompson draws our attention to reification, the purpose of which is to represent a transitory historical state of affairs as if it were permanent or natural, outside of time. One might suspect that Fox's attitude towards the green movement as the development of an ecological consciousness is very close to this. What is surely a contingent reaction to specific circumstances and can be explained in both sociological and psychological terms, is treated by Fox as the next essential stage in the evolution of the human race. This seems a highly dubious procedure.

We will now utilize Thompson's framework in order to highlight certain disturbing tendencies in Fox's work. We suggest that the force of this argument is cumulative. The fact that Fox seems to employ so many of these techniques should surely lead us to question the legitimacy of his overall project.

Legitimation

In *Original Blessing* Matthew Fox writes that, 'Living has something to do with Eros, love of life . . . Here lies wisdom.'[4] Here, as in so much of Fox, we have a communication problem. He redefines words and then uses them in his way. *Eros* is God, the hoping God, the erotic God. A God of play, pleasure and delight. It is a delightful picture that Fox paints, one of an intimate relationship with God in which we smile at each other. There is no sense of judgement, or of service or relationships with others, just me and God. His use of language is fresh and seems far from usual theology texts. He says what people want to hear and gives permission to enjoy life; he legitimates what I really want to do.

Agape is the word for love which is used in the New Testament. One must assume that, having three Greek words for love to choose from, the writers of the New Testament chose the one nearest to the meaning they wanted. *Agape* implies an open, sharing love while *eros* is more self seeking. Yet Fox redefines *eros* to mean compassion, 'interdependence'.[5]

When Fox talks about worship he says, 'Never be bored again. Create yourselves'.[6] He asks us to bring all that we have and are and continually to recreate our worlds. By implication, if we are bored and dry, then our worship is not real. He seems to have conveniently forgotten the experiences of the mystics he so often uses, of their 'dark night of the soul', when all does seem dark and empty. We were not created just for play and pleasure.

Eros is seen by C. S. Lewis as that which 'extenuates – almost sanctions – almost sanctifies any actions it leads

112

to.'[7] *Eros* is that which cannot be ignored and actions, seen by others as temptations, become duties – quasi-religious duties – around which a man-made religion evolves. Lewis warns of the danger of taking sexuality too seriously, of a 'reverential gravity' which attempts seriously to restore something like the phallic religion, a false god. Fox asks where men can go to recover their origins and comes up with the answer, 'To the sacredness of the *phallus*'.[8] He parallels the healing by Jesus on the Sabbath of the man born blind, which scandalized certain Jews, to the scandal which is bound to happen when sexuality is brought back to the realms of the sacred. He suggests that this will redress the imbalance caused by feminism.

Fox's use of legitimation is also seen in his use of the Bible. He substantiates each of his statements with a biblical reference and when one would suppose that he would suggest study of the Bible, or a recentering on it, he says that there can be no living worship if people have books, as it limits the movement of the body.[9]

Dissimulation

Fox believes that ecstasy offers a way to an experience 'beyond oneself', a taste of the divine.[10] It is a way of being out of control, of forgetting ourselves as we become a channel. In this way Fox redefines the effect of being 'out of control' through the use of drugs/drink as being of positive value. He says that what is needed for us to experience the ecstasy is for God to be released from our unconscious and so permeate our consciousness. He sees two kinds of ecstasy, natural and tactile: natural being nature, friendship, sex, arts, sports, tactile being chants, fasting, drugs, drink, all things which will open up the 'yes' faculties. Yet in *The Coming of the Cosmic Christ* he says that a civilization which denies the mystic will 'promote negative addictions: drugs, alcohol . . . It encourages us to seek outside stimulants to provide meaning for life.'[11] Which does he mean? The use of stimulants to provide ecstasy cannot be both positive and negative.

By contrast, John Powell says that to choose all available experiences is like trying to mix oil and water. The result is confusing, fragmenting, and disintegrating to the human person:

> To try to open himself to all possible experiences can only result in interior chaos; it would break him apart . . . If a person is determined to grow through contact with reality, which is the only way to grow, the experience of drunkenness or hallucinogenic narcotics will be very crippling to his personal growth. Becoming a person . . . involves the sacrificing of some experiences.[12]

Reification

Fox says that with the coming of the Cosmic Christ we will see the world in non-anthropocentric ways, and he criticizes Bultmann for his anthropocentric views: 'He [Bultmann] takes for granted that basically the center of gravity – the center from which all interpretation springs – is anthropology, the doctrine of man.'[13]

While he continues to criticize this view, for example criticizing the reordering of churches so that the priest at the altar now faces the people, which was introduced after the Second Vatican Council, as being anthropocentric and therefore 'essentially boring and lacking in mystery',[14] he then says that we have been 'loved from the beginning',[15] that this planet was not an accident, and that the universe 'wanted us and awaited us eagerly'. We are the ultimate creation and all that happened in the evolution of the universe was to enable our development. Isn't this view anthropocentric in the extreme?

He also uses the Gaia model to support the survival of humanity, not, as in the original model, to support the idea that some living things – not necessarily human – will survive. He says that decisions were made on our behalf – for example, the temperature of the earth has remained constant to enable our development to continue. He sees humanity as having evolved to become the nervous system of the earth and therefore the means by which nature will be saved.

Civil disobedience is cited as a way of recovering a sense of sacrifice in the worship of Western people: 'Those who dare to do civil disobedience . . . are worshipping in the ancient traditions of sacrifice.'[16] This is a most unusual way of using the word 'worship', one which serves his purpose as he uses it in a way he defines.

Unification

Fox takes pains to explain how mysticism has been misunderstood in the West;[17] that it has been felt to be a fad or something so difficult to do that only the very dedicated could attempt it. He also states that there is little study of the wisdom literature of the Old Testament, even by Christian ministers. What he says may be true for North America but his generalizations deny much of the study that takes place here. There has been an on-going tradition of uncomplicated mysticism through the experience of silence in Julian Groups, based on the example of Julian of Norwich – whom Fox often quotes, but not here.

Other traditions are omitted too. For example, he says 'mysticism . . . has never been tried on an ecumenical level. I cannot emphasize this fact enough.'[18] He defines 'mysticism' in this context as a depth of religious experience. One wonders if he has heard of the Taizé community where people of diverse faith, creeds and denominations live in community together, sharing in the silence and experiencing the mystery. I am sure others will have different examples of groups who have remained true to the mystical tradition. What Fox does is to put everyone together at the lowest level which might make people think, but is not very honest.

A further example of unification is his view of deep ecumenism, which is reminiscent of Karl Rahner's anonymous Christian, 'the reality of the Cosmic Christ who lives and breathes in Jesus and in *all* God's children, in all the prophets of religions everywhere, in all creatures of the universe.'[19]

Fragmentation

Fox encourages us to, 'Become a people. Gather together – you and your communities.'[20] He seems to want people to join together as Christ 'long(s) for harmony'.[21] He criticizes what he terms fall/redemption theology as being dualistic. In *Original Blessing* he gives a list of direct comparisons between creation-centred, both/and, and fall/redemption, either/or, theology, so making a division between what he sees as two different theologies.[22]

In so doing he is creating an artificial division, making an enemy 'out there'. Very little of value is seen in traditional Christianity, yet he agrees with Anthony Stevens that, 'the act of scapegoating is "obscene"'. He continues, 'Unhealthy people try to conceal their own shadows by "rationalising" to justify what they do and say . . . The cause of scapegoating . . . is that feelings experienced by the ego are regarded as too dangerous to deal with.'[23]

The young are advised to 'start (their) own culture'[24] as adults have made such a mess of the world that they have nothing to teach them, so causing another division in what he sees as a divided world. He gives no insight as to how

116

these gaps could be bridged, nor does he seem to realize that they too could turn into groups which have a scapegoat – adults.

Conclusion

Our main concern with Fox is that he is ultimately not radical enough. Although his work represents an attempt to revitalise elements of the Christian tradition which appear amenable to an ecological stance, the end product is a confusing collage of disparate and even conflicting ideas. In his eagerness to create a new theological paradigm he constructs an unworkable framework.

This failure is, in itself, instructive. If we can identify where Fox is going wrong it may then be possible to envisage what a workable structure might include. The danger of Fox's approach is its romantic appeal to what are invariably reactions to the natural world which originate from unconscious sources. His use of images, symbols and ritual is essentially unreflective and uncritical. Rather than trying to incorporate human reason and then move beyond it, he by-passes it altogether. Rationality is seen as the enemy, the destroyer of the harmony between humanity and the natural world. By appealing to the senses alone he suggests we can return to the Garden of Eden. Unfortunately, Eden is not so easily regained.

This refusal to take account of human powers of reason and reflection merely leaves us with an emotional backlash against scientific and technological thought. The political implications of this are immense and frightening. Previously such approaches have led to National Socialism in the Germany of the 1930s and had echoes in the more recent horror of Cambodia. A naive return to nature omits too much truth about humanity and opens a channel for a darker side to enter unobserved and unchallenged.

If there is a way back to Eden – and that is an open question – it must be through the fire of human reason and with a recognition that humanity is not yet what it shall be. Hence the need for an ideology critique. Fox represents not progress, but regression, a potential unleashing of unconscious forces that are as likely to destroy as to recreate. Progress – finding ways of living peacefully with each other and our neighbour, the natural world – require at least a reasoned and reflective attempt to come to terms with ourselves. Less than this will not suffice.

Notes

1. This account is based on a lecture given by Matthew Fox in his series in the UK in 1990. This particular lecture was given at Thornbury Parish Church just outside Bristol on 10 July.
2. See, for instance, Don Cupitt, *The New Christian Ethics* (SCM Press 1988), p. 8.
3. The following section is based upon John B. Thompson, *Ideology and Modern Culture* (Polity Press 1990), pp. 56–67.
4. Matthew Fox, *Original Blessing* (Santa Fe, NM, Bear & Co. Inc., 1983), p. 9.
5. Matthew Fox, *The Coming of the Cosmic Christ* (San Francisco, Harper & Row, 1988), p. 33.
6. Fox, p. 229.
7. C. S. Lewis, *The Four Loves* (Collins 1968), p. 103.
8. Fox, p. 176.
9. Fox, p. 217.
10. Matthew Fox, *Whee! We,wee. All the Way Home* (Santa Fe, NM, Bear & Co. Inc., 1985), p. 47.
11. Fox, *The Coming of the Cosmic Christ*, p. 43.
12. John Powell SJ, *Unconditional Love* (Texas, Argus Communications, 1978), p. 49.
13. Fox, p. 78.
14. Fox, p. 212.
15. Fox, p. 228.
16. Fox, p. 226.

17. Fox, pp. 41–44.
18. Fox, p. 229.
19. Fox, p. 7.
20. Fox, p. 228.
21. Fox, p. 244.
22. Fox, *Original Blessing*, pp. 316–19.
23. Fox, *The Coming of the Cosmic Christ*, p. 208.
24. Fox, p. 198.

6

'Sing An Old-Fashioned Song . . . Travel on down the road to long-ago'
(1930s song)

IAN BALL

In recent years it has been widely accepted that if any organization is to be considered dynamic, then it should be seen to be responding to relevant social issues. Thus the church, like any half-decent educational institution, should be actively engaged in assisting people in their struggle to express and activate their environmental concerns. Therefore in this chapter I propose to consider some examples of church-based literature and activity that has been produced in response to the issue of 'the environment'.

The debate by some theologians has been vigorous and there has been a recognition that the issue of the environment has wide implications:

> I find one can't talk about this simply in the abstract because Christian attitudes, Christian theology is and always has been deeply affected by context . . . You can't just talk about the integrity of creation by itself without recognising that this has deep social and political implications.[1]

Unfortunately most of the widely available, 'popular', material on the subject is at best unadventurous.

In *God is Green* Ian Bradley lays his case out very clearly: 'This book seeks to show that the Christian faith is intrinsically green . . .',[2] and he then works towards demonstrating his belief through a use of scripture and other authorities, ancient and modern. The general tone of the book does suggest that it is designed for a largely 'confessing' readership. It would seem to be intended to assist those who are within the church to feel confident in relating their church and environmental interests. The church has often seemed to need such texts. I remember one from my childhood: 'Is pop music Christian?', curious texts only of use for those who need to place everything they do under the control of one aspect of their lives. These works are essentially unchallenging, and in Bradley's case inclined towards meaningless platitude, as in the title. They simply assemble texts, usually taken at face value, and consider that, with a few helpful hints for those in power (in this case the Church Commissioners),[3] the problem has been successfully encountered. The questions that arise from a reading of Bradley's book are not so much related to what is in the book, but to those who feel a need to possess it.

Another recent book is *Green Christianity* by Tim Cooper. This somewhat confused production aims to explore, 'the inter-connections between Christianity and ecology. My intention is to develop a Christian view of the whole creation which is appropriate to an industrialised world very different from that of over two thousand years ago'.[4] Given that desire, it is strange that the book relies on the usual approach of quoting texts whose origin is even more ancient, though at times somewhat remarkably reinterpreted: 'The Bible calls us to be earth's caretakers' (p. 53)! So we are, I suppose, those who open and close the earth, carrying the keys to heaven and hell as well. The book is something of a lesson, in that the writer, having committed himself to the Grand Design quoted above (and, it seems, in so doing is providing a fine example of 'the human problem' with which he is attempting to concern himself), stumbles around without much understanding of the many subject areas encountered. The tone of the book suggests that the writer is desperate to find Christian companions for his 'green' journey.

Underneath the confusion there is an important point to discern. It is that the author has realized (passionately) that we all need to do something about the growing problems humans have assisted in creating. The writer is being driven by the need to do something . . . and that has come first. Right action to the fore, the theology second. The book begins not with religion but with the greens: – *'Green Christianity* is written in the firm conviction that the green movement's growing influence represents a bright ray of hope in a world where . . .'[5] Though the book illustrates the manner in which enthusiasts of one kind or another can 'take over' institutions, it also illustrates the way we humans are: creatures able to identify problems, deal with them directly and then provide the justification . . .

Thus the book also illustrates the manner in which religions change. Like every other institution they are in the end subject to the effects of social and intellectual change. An ability to recognize that effect and to work with it would make churches much more effective social institutions – not in order to take over others, but simply to assist others in their particular search for meaning and significance. In that recognition could lie a discovery of the message of hope that Tim Cooper seems to imply lies more with the 'greens' than with religion.

Given the attention that environmental matters now receive it is reasonable to expect some official response in the recent Archbishop's Commission on Rural Areas (ACORA) report, *Faith in the Countryside*.[6] The ACORA report is based in part on visits to many localities. It seeks

122

to listen, consider and respond. It lays out a role for the
professional clergy that requires them 'To be aware of the
mission . . . To share in vision . . . To focus on what can
and should be done'.[7] It recognizes that the vision of the
church needs to go beyond merely human concerns, and
claims (somewhat presumptuously?) that, 'the ecological
debate is at heart a theological one and needs to be accepted
as such by the church at large, and not just by those in
rural areas or with a particular environmental concern.'[8] It
suggests that the mission of the church should include
asserting 'the cosmic significance of the Gospel',[9] a curious
and unexplained statement that is presumably intended to
imply something of an environmental concern.

Yet whilst the report clearly recognizes that there are
environmental issues, it never concerns itself with anything
more than the human element. Even the chapter which
contains the words, 'this [environmental concern] has been
a spontaneous, indeed religious, recognition of humanity's
deep relatedness to the rest of nature', is called 'The
Environment and *Rural Development*'.[10] One needs no
great imagination to guess which species features in that!
Maybe the very factual and human-centred nature of the
report is an indication of its theology.

As with so much of the so-called Christian writing
relating to the environmental theme there is a greater
emphasis on the Old Testament than the New (at an
approximate ratio of two to one). In establishing its
theology of personhood, the document performs an amazing
act: 'The Commission has gone in a different direction for
its theology of the person. In fact, it begins with a rejection
of the post-Enlightenment view of human autonomy and
reasserts a biblical position of humankind created in the
image of God'.[11] Though it has attempted a summary of
the rise of individualism, to dismiss such views with sleight
of hand does seem somewhat extreme. Surely there is more
to be considered in the 'post-Enlightenment view' than two

123

pages of a report will allow? But maybe there would be some justification if what was being presented really did advance matters; but which biblical view is called up? Why, Genesis, of course. The report even tries to suggest that Genesis 2 ('It is not good that the man should be alone, I will make a helper fit for him') presents sexual equality: 'This account of the creation of human community is of a man and woman: the image of God as male and female, inextricably bound to make up the fullness of human personhood.'[12] Now, it might be possible to suggest that there is a recognition of the need for some sort of balance. But to say, 'this account', is to bring in the whole story. Can this curious reinterpretation of an image of male dominance be presented to the twentieth century with any real seriousness?

It may be argued that the Genesis issue is of little importance to environmental matters. However that would be to ignore the effect of self-imaging on our behaviour patterns. It does matter that we try and assess the effect of past views such as the so-called 'Enlightenment project.' It does matter that we explore other views of humanity. But the church must recognize more openly that we are not going to achieve very much simply by twisting ancient texts. Society deserves better than that.[13]

It would seem that 'Faith in The Countryside' represents another example of the stresses that can be put on an organization such as the church. The report has to be in a language that is acceptable to those who exercise power in the land. Criticisms of policy are acceptable, though they may be ignored; but unless they are in an appropriate form they will not even be noticed. 'Market place economics' and other such consumptionist theories are in the ascendant and we all have to work with its language; and the language we are allowed controls what we can say.[14]

There have, of course, been other responses than those mentioned.[15] But most of the really prophetic work comes from outside the church.[16] Viewed from outside it seems strange that the members of a major institution should feel so obliged to justify themselves by constant reference to the quasi-metaphysical speculations of nomadic tribesmen of the second millennium BC!

On a practical level the major response by the Christian churches has been stimulated by a secular organization, namely through the establishment of the Network on Conservation and Religion by the World Wide Fund for Nature. Employing a multi-faith approach, the Network has encouraged individuals and groups to join in expressing their concerns. It has collected an amazing variety of supporters and has reported on a wide variety of activities relating to ecology and environment. WWF has been the major promoter of events within the church by actively encouraging and publishing liturgies that assist with the process of attitudinal change. There have been problems. First, the events and activities have been promoted in a somewhat hierarchical fashion. This has led to the production of material through cathedrals with a dissemination 'downwards'. The use of a cathedral does give authority to what is being done, but, as occurred with the Salisbury Creation Festival of May 1990, this means that the event is capable of being ignored by those within the diocese who are away from the centre of events. Nonetheless, the liturgies produced at Winchester and Coventry have been widely used by interested church groups and have greatly assisted in stimulating an interest and in channelling concern.

Second, the approach of using prepared liturgies and conferences is in itself limiting. The need is not just to provide material for digestion: that is, once again, to follow the attitude of there being authority 'out there' to which one defers. It is easy then for some to become the 'experts' who pronounce judgment. The old pattern of handing over our responsibility to others is continued, the listener can be

125

merely passive and the 'expert' or the liturgy just another branch of the entertainment business – admittedly, in this case a rather exciting one. How exciting and confirming to have the wonderful sonority of a cathedral liturgy to reinforce our concern. But ultimately the experience is only passive. It may stimulate some to change people's lives, following a conversion, but that is insufficient for what society, with all its problems, requires. People need to be active in their explorations of issues.

A further problem has been the nature of the Christian response. So much has been stimulated by WWF in the years since their great Assisi gathering in 1986 that it would be impossible to review it easily. One of the effects has been a stimulating of the debate about the nature of Christianity. This was presumably not an original intention, as WWF is primarily concerned with conservation issues. It was certainly something of a shock for some of those involved, and illustrates the dangers for any organization when it innocently begins to treat with something as complex as a religion.

In the process of this debate, sides were clearly taken and the impression left on some non-church people was a considerable distaste for Christianity caused by the insidious and vitriolic attempts made by some extremists in their attempts to disrupt the Canterbury Festival of Faith and the Environment in September 1989. Many participants were horrified by the howling mob of 'Christian' objectors that greeted the three multi-faith pilgrimages at the start of the festival. It was fairly evident that some of those who led the objections were more interested in self-publicity than in their claims to be protecting the faith. The objectors did clearly show how important it is that those wishing to see a dynamic faith should engage in constructing processes that will enable that to happen. The objectors at Canterbury had a certain

126

logic on their side. Religious truth is either partial and changing, or it isn't. If it is a 'once and for ever' revelation, then the objectors have a point.

The WWF effort to energize the churches into considering environmental issues illustrates the struggle for influence. What was a laudable (and largely successful) attempt to introduce some new thinking on an important issue, created an interesting conflict. The process interested those who have fanciful romantic notions of a return to their particular vision of an 'ecologically sound' past, people who seem prepared to grasp at almost any 'alternative'. There were also those who see their vision in biblical and fundamentalist terms and who similarly wish for a state of simple purity. There were 'green' and biblical fundamentalists both wanting the same result: power to effect their particular views. Well, we have had theocratic states, and they have usually been good examples of tyranny. So it would be in a world ruled by any single interest group, no matter how morally appealing the message. We are emerging from such a period in Europe. The apparent human desire for power requires us to struggle for plurality.

If, then, the response of the church towards environmentalism is considered to be somewhat limited, what is to be done to improve matters? In attempting to find an answer one inevitably becomes linked to a wider consideration of the manner in which the church operates. That becomes a basic question: 'What is the church for'?

Once upon a time, and almost certainly in a never-never land, the church seemed to provide the whole context for life. But now we who are involved in the church are just another section of society. Given that scripture seems so definite at times – 'no one can come to the Father except through me' – we have to struggle with the implications of the realization that the church does not provide all the answers. Yet so much of church life and liturgy continues as if it is providing everything. If the church is to be anything other than a cosy refuge from the storm of modernity, it needs to accept the principle of change, of life within the flux.

Part of that acceptance means an opening up of minds and structures to what those outside may be saying . . . and it's an awfully big world out there. This 'opening up' should not be seen simply in terms of receiving or taking. Despite the apparent lack of membership, there is still a desire amongst many to see the churches actively involved in society. In my very rural part of Britain the local churches still occupy an important position in local life. People will allow them to wither and seem to operate happily enough without them. But should a particular church wish to develop a more active and open community role, then this is easily accepted by locals and newcomers alike. I do not believe that there is anything particularly 'rural' about this attitude.

There are many, both religious and non-religious, who agonize about the present seeming confusion of human purpose. Many regret our emptiness in a world in which we seem to want for nothing. Will we witness greater exploitation, a rampant consumerism: a 'commodity fetishism', relieved only by various forms of romanticism? Or is it possible for society to create new possibilities for itself? To explore priorities, engage in activity that, whilst accepting the transitory nature of humanity, provides meaning in ways that do not require exploitation of each other and the rest of creation? The church surely has a role to play in assisting this process. In its various forms it has a huge potential, much greater than, I suspect, many realize. The church exists at all levels of society and possesses a vast range of talents and physical resources. What often seems lacking is a sense of confidence in developing a role that is not just self-satisfying. Further, unlike many other 'lifeworlds', in order to justify itself to itself it actually has to be concerned with those who are not within the group. Why, oh why cannot it boldly embrace the void?

Notes

1. Archbishop of York, British Council of Churches Conference, Canterbury Festival of Faith and the Environment, September 1989.
2. Ian Bradley, *God is Green* (Darton, Longman & Todd 1990), p. 1.
3. Bradley, p. 111.
4. Tim Cooper, *Green Christianity* (Spire/Hodder and Stoughton 1990), p. 2.
5. Cooper, p. 1ff.
6. *Faith in the Countryside* (Churchman 1990).
7. *Faith in the Countryside*, para 8.19, p. 147.
8. *Faith in the Countryside*, para 8.11, p. 144.
9. Expressed in the paragraph referred to above as 'fifth mission aim' in addition to the four outlined by the 1988 Lambeth Conference.
10. *Faith in the Countryside*, para 4.3, p. 35.
11. *Faith in the Countryside*, para 2.39, p. 20.
12. *Faith in the Countryside*, para 2.40.
13. In the January 1991 edition of *Theology* David Jenkins in a review of Don Cupitt's *Radicals and the Future of the Church* asks, 'I wonder where we go from here?'. Unless the church is prepared to become more creative in its thinking, the answer will be, 'Nowhere'.
14. It is not just reports such as that of ACORA that seem to find difficulty in expressing themselves. Recent government policy initiatives in education are producing a similar effect. The National Curriculum has 'squeezed' time available for creative subjects; art, for example, is often placed under 'design and technology'. It is proving very difficult to find time for local creative initiatives as the problems are compounded by the various dictates that emanate from the frozen imaginations of those in power.
    Further to that are the emphases being made in the way courses are presented to potential students. One recent prospectus, advertising an economics course starts, 'In life, to get what you want you have to spend money . . . Economics is about how you go

about satisfying your wants and needs, and how society provides for you.'

15. The American theologian Elizabeth Dodson Gray, interviewed in *Resurgence* (Nov/Dec 1990), has severely criticized the Christian response to environmentalism as a 'new version of "dominion".' She stresses the need to reject dominion: 'Why do we have such a hard time giving up this theological error [in Genesis]? Why are we such intellectual cowards? . . . I know scarcely anyone who is working on what it means to say as a Christian, "We are within life on this planet and not above; we are not rulers of this life-system".'

16. See, for instance, works like Rachel Carson's *Silent Spring* and, more recently, James Lovelock's Gaia Hypothesis: 'When I wrote the first book on Gaia I had no inkling that it would be taken as a religious book' (*The Ages of Gaia*, p. 203).

Part Three

7

Creating Spaces

MARGARET GOODALL and JOHN READER

In recent years there has been an almost constant flow of literature in the field of green theology. As a reaction to the awareness of a potential ecological crisis this is perhaps necessary. However, the exact nature of Christianity's response to this question requires critical examination. At one extreme are those who merely wish to appropriate the Christian tradition to the green movement, probably in order to give it wider legitimation. At the other lies an unwillingness even to consider the need for new interpretations despite an acknowledgement of the ecological issues.[1] How should Christianity be responding to the environmental question?

It was with this in mind that we began to review the work of such authors as Sean McDonagh, Matthew Fox and Jürgen Moltmann. It soon became clear that one fundamental weakness of this material is its failure to provide adequate spaces for the process of theological reflection. In other words, instead of allowing possible responses to emerge from an open discussion between Christianity, ecology and other disciplines, it falls into the trap of imposing Christian answers before the questions have even been posed.

At the end of May 1990 a two day conference was held in Northamptonshire to debate the World Council of

133

Churches guidelines on 'Justice, Peace and the Integrity of Creation'. Our reflections upon this presentation led us to the conclusion that the subject of creating space was itself worthy of further investigation. For instance, one of the roles of New Social Movements (referred to hereafter as NSMs), as described by Alberto Melucci,[2] has been to create new public spaces for the discussion of moral and political issues. However, the same need for spaces is encountered in counselling, where the relationship between client and counsellor seeks to provide the context for deeper exploration of the individual personality. Having recognized the interdisciplinary nature of the study of creating spaces we began to pursue various lines of thought. What follows is an attempt to present some of those which we feel are particularly illuminating.

The style of this chapter reflects the way that we decided to work. Rather than covering the same ground twice or trying to produce an agreed statement we have chosen to present this as two distinct voices in conversation. The pattern which emerged was that Margaret would play the initial theme from within the perspective of her own involvement in both ministry and counselling and that John would take up the variations from the disciplines of philosophy and sociology. Another way of describing this would be to say that Margaret begins from the personal and John from the political. One of the challenges of this whole enterprise is to hold these two worlds in relationship. Hence the way in which we have worked is itself part of what we want to say.

Margaret's interest in the ecological debate began by reading green literature published by both secular and religious organizations. I found that although full of information and very persuasive it failed to do the one thing that seemed necessary: to change my attitude. The material was dealing with specific localized details and assuming the answers, not allowing the space for ideas to be internalized. If the ecological debate is concerned with changing attitudes then the space must be found for greater discussion to take place. I was also uneasy with the choice of symbols used in the literature, for example, the earth as 'home' or 'family', both ideas which suggest a form of romanticism and presuppose that we already have the answers.

There is also talk of a battle with nature, in which humanity thinks of itself as an outside force destined to conquer and dominate, rather than experiencing itself as part of nature. E. F. Schumacher suggests that this is because we are 'inclined to treat as valueless everything that we have not made ourselves'.[3] It is because humanity has been so successful in its industrial activity that pollution, environment and ecology have so suddenly become household words. We have begun to realize that the world's resources are not limitless and that the wonder fuel, nuclear power, will leave problems of contamination for generations. There is a sense of desperation resulting from information about what we have done to the earth and projections of what will happen if we do not change how we relate to it. But where can we go to find hope? Change is often painful and humanity would rather that things continue as they are. As Archbishop Thomas à Becket says in T. S. Eliot's play, *Murder in the Cathedral*: 'Human kind cannot bear very much reality'.[4] So, ways are found to escape from the situation. People can drop out into the counter-cultures, put their trust in science and technology for the answers, or become dependent upon work, the family, the stock market, drugs, the occult, anything which gives a point of reference and an identity in what has become an impersonal world of computers and 'PIN numbers'.

May it not be the case, then, that Christianity's main contribution is not so much, at first, in terms of content, which may only encourage forms of escapism, but rather through the spaces or the opportunities that it can create for the conduct of the debate? In order for discussions to happen, two things are necessary. First, a discourse which is capable of expressing the ideas or the feelings that people need to articulate. Second, times and places where these discussions can occur. This may sound strange or obvious in a society which takes democratic freedoms for granted, but the existence of a parliamentary democracy does not in itself guarantee the opportunities for the free expression of views on all subjects.[5] People have to be able to meet, to be able to feel that the discussion of environmental concerns as a moral issue is legitimate, and they must share enough of a common language for such discussion to make sense.

The need for legitimation was highlighted by the impact of Mrs Thatcher's speech on the environment in 1988, which marked the beginning of the subject as a serious topic for political debate in Britain. Unfortunately, because it was made within the context and discourse of political economy, rather than within the setting of deeper human concerns, it still denied a convincing moral dimension to the issues. It is in this area, perhaps, that the Christian tradition in this country has something to offer, given both its resources of language and its potential for creating spaces for the enabling of the debate.

In order to give greater support to this argument, it is important to examine awareness of the means of creating spaces as it arises in the human sciences. The purpose of this is not just to illustrate the legitimacy of the study, but to sharpen the focus for theology. Has Christianity been aware of the power that it can exercise through the spaces that it creates? Certainly, one can now see this at work explicitly in the influence that the churches have had over recent events in Eastern Europe, where they have been for so long a potential focus for any debate on alternative political approaches. However, the situation in Britain is far less clear. Here there are other agencies meeting such needs and there is no consensus within Christianity itself on involvement in political issues. There is thus a need to look carefully and critically at current operations to examine how this potential is being utilized – if at all – and at what factors govern the ways in which the churches use the space they create. Listening to the insights of other disciplines is one method of establishing such a critical perspective.

The acceptance of change and the need for spaces

Within the church

It was during a visit to what was until recently East Germany that Margaret realized what the church can provide. In three small villages around Leipzig the church was offering people a place in which to talk about the society in which they lived. The congregations took a risk in expressing their feelings, but within the church they felt safe. They had been given the confidence and the space to explore ideas and even to talk tentatively of change. These were ordinary people who, a few months later, were to become part of the group which marched by candlelight for the legalisation of the New Forum opposition. The rallies started as a protest march of a few thousand following a prayer meeting and grew into a spontaneous mass event which proved to be a major force for change.

The church offered them the freedom to criticize society from within an organization which gives hope through the continuity of its tradition, its language, ritual and symbolism. It is able to point us towards something beyond ourselves and, in so doing, it offers a perspective from which to debate wider issues. Through rites of passage – baptism, confirmation, marriage and funerals – the church gives a way of concretizing changes which have to be made as we go through life. By using a set form it gives the perspective of continuity and enables the transition from one stage to another. Change can be threatening because we like what is familiar, but if people refuse to change then growth is stunted and personalities become deformed. The church can allow for the possibility of change because of the belief that people can experience the transforming love of God, which makes them part of a new creation. Christianity depends upon the call to repent and this can offer an openness to the possibility of change. Once accepted by the individual, this may become the basis for greater awareness of and greater flexibility on wider issues.

Liturgy is the vehicle through which worship is expressed and creates an environment in which human beings can confront those sides of themselves which, under normal circumstances, they dare not face. Many people live in a state of fear which either makes them run away from each other, or cling to each other in desperation, so forming a clique in which to feel safe and from which to be suspicious of others. Both states of being rob the person of the free space in which to grow by limiting contact with strangeness. Worship contains both positive and negative elements which allow us to make sense of the polarities within ourselves. It would seem that the problem with the environmental literature holds true for thought about the person. If everything is so open and known, why still does nothing change? One answer is that we refuse to acknowledge the shadow side of our nature and that, until we do, we will be less than whole.

John Sanford offers an example of the importance of this in his interpretation of the parable of the Good Samaritan.[6] He suggests that as in dreams we play more than one part, so the person being robbed is ourself. The priest and the Levite who walk past are the respectable sides of our nature who are unable to do anything to save us. The Good Samaritan is the unacceptable part of our personality, yet it is that which has the power to save and to restore wholeness. But, to explore that part of ourselves that is considered dangerous means taking a risk. Jim Cotter in his book *Prayers at Night*[7] bids us go into the 'depths of our being', that we may be given the freedom to grow by entering into our darkness.

One of the characteristics of being fully human is to recognize our dependence on each other. The community of the church could be seen as a bridge between the private world of self and home and the public world, where individuals might experience a shared common space and learn what inter-dependence means in practice, allowing the space for the healing of both inner and outer worlds. Inter-dependence is a concept which has come to the centre of the environmental debate as a way of describing our relationship with the rest of the natural order. For example, the destruction of the rain forests has been shown to be of the utmost importance to humanity as it has a direct effect on the earth's weather systems. We are not free to do as we wish with the earth's resources, as all our actions affect other parts of the natural world.

Within society

John's first encounter with the concept of the open space, or the clearing, was in Martin Heidegger's later philosophy. In his search for an alternative to traditional understandings of truth, Heidegger proposes that truth is something that occurs or happens. He presents the image of walking through a forest and then suddenly coming upon a clearing:

> In the midst of beings as a whole an open place occurs. There is a clearing, a lighting. Thought of in reference to what is, to beings, this clearing is in a greater degree than are beings. This open centre is therefore not surrounded by what is; rather the lighting centre itself encircles all that is.[8]

139

There is no need to become deeply involved in the intricacies of Heidegger's work to recognize the significance of this idea. I have already suggested elsewhere that it enables pastoral theology to reach a fuller understanding of the nature of human communication.[9] If Heidegger is correct, then our supposed control of language is an illusion. Authentic contact with others occurs not through our deliberate and calculating use of speech, but only when there is an open space within which truth can be revealed.

The weakness of this attractive approach is that it can lead to an unacceptable subjectivity. It is surely not the case that human beings stumble into these metaphorical clearings and then have to wait for moments of revelation in order for insight and communication to occur. However, neither is it the case that humans are fully in control of this process – to go to the opposite extreme. It is important that Heidegger draws this to our attention.

We exercise limited control of communication through language, moving in a realm which is neither fully subjective nor fully objective. This can be described as an open space within which there is always freedom of interpretation and the possibility of new meaning. If this were not the case, all discussions would be settled in advance. This is a valuable and helpful insight which steers us towards further investigation. Is it possible to identify such spaces in society and to examine how they operate?

In order to answer this we turn from philosophy to sociology. Some early work of Jürgen Habermas provides important evidence. 'Strukturwandel der Offentlichkeit', published in Germany in 1962, has only recently been translated into English, reflecting a growing interest in Habermas' work.[10] The book shows the development and subsequent decline of what he calls the bourgeois public sphere, which we might describe as the spaces within which open political debate took place. Once again, there

140

is a wealth of material here which it is not within our brief to investigate, but Habermas' main contribution for our purposes is his examination of the ways in which certain places and institutions functioned as spaces for debate and then lost that function as capitalist society developed. For instance, he draws attention to the one-time importance of writing letters as an outlet for open discussion.[11] Salons, clubs and reading houses fulfilled a vital role in providing meeting places where such discussions could be carried further. This changed, as families in particular became more deeply engaged in capitalist production and home life became more clearly differentiated both from work and from political concerns. The notion of family privacy, now so taken for granted, may be seen as a relatively recent development, stemming from the requirements of a society switching its main energies into the production of goods and services. The result was a loss of contact with formal political debate, which then also became more specialized:

> The shrinking of the private sphere into the inner areas of a conjugal family largely relieved of function and weakened in authority . . . provided only the illusion of a perfectly private personal sphere; for to the extent that private people withdrew from their socially-controlled roles as property owners into the purely 'personal' ones of their non-committal use of leisure time, they came directly under the influence of semi-public authorities, without the protection of an institutionally protected domestic domain. Leisure behaviour supplies the key to the floodlit privacy of the new sphere, to the externalisation of what is declared to be the inner life.[12]

In other words, there is a redefinition of the boundaries between 'public' and 'private' which actually works to the detriment of open political discussion. That which had previously taken place publicly but informally could now only occur in private, behind the closed doors of the family

141

abode. What public discussion remained had then to become more formal and thus more subject to external control.

Habermas' historical and sociological investigation illustrates the importance of open public spaces if debate is to occur. It leaves us with the question of where such spaces might be found in contemporary British society. As so much so-called open public debate is in fact set up and controlled by the media, how useful is it when it comes to the discussion of new and controversial topics? There are at least two questions to consider. First, to what extent is any such debate subject to purely commercial criteria? Second, given the inevitable political influences over the media, how dangerous is it to attribute to such debates any degree of objectivity or neutrality? We may assume that much of the open discussion that does happen, even within what is a democratic setting, is a long way from meeting the needs of people to talk about environmental issues, for instance, on a deeper level.

It is at this stage that we need to examine the development of what are now being called New Social Movements (NSMs). Although the term originates from the work of the French sociologist Alain Touraine,[13] it has now been adopted and taken further by both Habermas and Melucci.[14] As ever, Habermas offers a more theoretical perspective, with its attendant limitations, so we will rely instead upon Melucci, who has had the advantage of having carried out empirical research upon groups who fall into this category. Specific examples would be the peace movement, the women's movement and the environmental movement. The use of the word 'movement' suggests rather too coherent and definite a picture of what is in fact a complex area of social action. One of Melucci's virtues is that he recognizes this and is concerned not to present a false image of what is happening. The particular aspect of his research that is of greatest interest reveals that one of the aims and effects of this new form of social activity is to create new spaces for the public debate of political and moral issues:

> The emerging forms of collective action differ from conventional models of political organisation and operate increasingly outside the established parameters of the political system. In complex societies collective action creates new spaces which function as a genuine sub-system. These social spaces are the products of different forms of behaviour which the system is unable to integrate.[15]

The theory is that suppression of open discussion relating to issues of deep personal concern – for instance, our relationships with each other or with the natural world – either through deliberate intent or through the normal exercise of power within society, will not finally prevent these questions from surfacing. At the moment their main outlet is these new forms of collective action.

Rather than seeking formal organization, they operate through a system of networks. Individuals and groups take advantage of greater mobility and new information technology to remain in contact with others of a similar persuasion in other parts of the country and indeed across national boundaries. There is a conscious attempt to steer clear of the normal channels of power and traditional methods of organization in order to work beneath the surface of established political institutions. One of the great advantages of this approach is that it can bring to the surface the networks of power that are already in operation, without becoming drawn into them. It is vital to render power visible, because otherwise it is not possible to identify who is responsible for the goals of social life. If it can be made clear who is making which decisions and in whose interests they are being made, then it is at least possible to begin to change this process. Once more, this demands the creation of new spaces within which power can be brought to the surface and then challenged.

I have argued elsewhere that a number of Christian groups are now beginning to adopt this style of collective action.[16] It is not surprising that they tend to be those groups most closely associated with existing NSMs. It seems that a greater awareness of current analyses of NSMs would be of benefit to these groups. It would then be possible to give realistic answers to such questions as how effective they are likely to be. Under what conditions do such groups operate successfully? Do they possess any real potential for political change, or will they be swallowed up by the system they aim to oppose? Such answers would provide a sounder base for what is important and necessary Christian involvement in these areas. They would also raise further questions about contemporary church organization and its possible limitations in the face of new challenges. Perhaps a greater willingness to organize more flexibly and informally, combined with more imaginative use of the language and symbols within the tradition, would equip the churches to make a more vital and effective contribution to the environmental debate. Examples of good practice established in the community are to be found in the following chapters of this book.

The renewal of vision and hope

James Fowler was the guest speaker at a Faith Development conference in Nottingham in June 1990 and while talking about Parker Palmer's book *The Company of Strangers*,[17] he gave this definition of the word 'campus'. In medieval times the campus was a place where those in dispute could come to find a safe place for discussion. Weapons would be left outside the area, thus limiting the damage that could be created. The word is now used to describe the grounds of an educational institution, but, like the word 'school', it has lost the idea of openness which was part of its original meaning. 'Schola'[18] meant a place of leisure where one could come away from the business of life to discover its mysteries, but education has become so pressurised that the spaces have now been lost. The emphasis is upon productivity and education is the arena for the hectic race to accomplish.

Where can ordinary people find a place for 'exploring the mysteries' where they will not feel threatened and damage will be limited? As Salman Rushdie says, there needs to be space for the different voices to be heard, although he sees literature especially as fulfilling that function:

> Literature is the one place in any society where, within the secrecy of our own heads, we can hear voices talking about everything in every possible way. The reason for ensuring that that privileged arena is preserved . . . is that we, all of us, readers and writers and citizens and generals and godmen, need that little unimportant-looking room. We do not need to call it sacred, but we do need to remember that it is necessary.[19]

Perhaps a time of education is needed for people to recognize the importance of open spaces and how to use them. Legislation for 'time off' does not work, as many people do not know how to use their leisure time. To be gainfully employed is seen as a necessity. Thomas Merton wrote, 'What will people say if I spend my time watching the rain instead of enjoying myself?'[20] Having fun has become compulsory. It is a fact of modern life that most family arguments happen on a Sunday, and most family murders on a Sunday evening. Time is something that must be filled, leaving no space for the imagination to explore or to recognize the mysteries. Moltmann writes that God's final act, completing the work of creation, was

145

to rest, to look at what had been done and to enjoy it. The Sabbath is the only Jewish festival that is not dependent on salvation history: it is a free gift.[21]

The world has become for many a place of no hope. While the nuclear threat may appear to have receded, that of an imminent ecological disaster has become only too real. So, for those who can see no hope, the answer is to enjoy the present and, in so doing, to create debt for the future. Hope is essential, as anxiety can be debilitating and despair can lead to a paralysis of the will. There is a need to create new spaces or to change the expectations of the ones we have. What is heard is partly dependent upon where it is heard. We hear and we forget because we do not understand. If we can learn to use images and symbols which make connections with both sides of the brain, then we will engage the whole personality, so that what is experienced becomes concrete, rooted in our own experience.

If Christianity was to acknowledge the importance of creating spaces it would be very tempting for it to fall into the assumption that the process could be carried out in an unambiguous fashion. Thus the instant and appropriate reaction to the emergence of any new moral dilemma would be merely to create the possibility of an open discussion. The task would then be largely complete. However, such an assumption would be mistaken as it fails to take into account the nature of power as it operates in this area. For insights into this we turn to the work of Michel Foucault.

His early historical study into the development of disciplinary institutions, notably of prisons and hospitals,[22] revealed the complexity of the networks of power which underlay the control of space so vital for their operation. The design and organization of these institutions, as they developed from the seventeenth century onwards, represented attempts to fit human beings into discrete orders and categories in order to facilitate their surveillance and control. Each person is allotted a space within a grid so that they can be carefully observed. All of the space within a confined area must be ordered; there should be no waste, no gaps, no free margins; nothing should escape.

Perhaps the primary example of this was Bentham's Panopticon, which although never fully implemented, became the model for many prisons. Its central viewing point gave visual access to all spaces and corners of the prisoners' block. We can recognize similar ideas at work in the design of contemporary office buildings and shopping arcades. Often there are deliberately no private spaces, no corners or alleyways. All must remain open to full public view. The interesting question is whether such design merely reflects a fully worked-out philosophy of humanity or whether it is rather a part of an historical development with no such conscious plan, but which nevertheless encourages that philosophy. Foucault's view would be closer to the latter. He does not see power as something which some people possess and some do not, but rather as a network of relationships in which all are involved, even those who are apparently powerless. There is only power and counterpower.[23] It is impossible to destroy power and it can often only be altered by local resistance.

This has important implications for the churches' employment and creation of spaces. Churches are already part of existing networks of power and would be foolish to delude themselves that they are ever only part of a resistance movement. Thus, even attempts to create new spaces for public debate could never be unambiguous. This seems an illuminating insight into church life. What messages about the relationship with local power structures are conveyed, for instance, by family pews in rural churches? What is communicated by the ordering of church council meetings, the places where they meet, the arrangement of the seating and so on? Even attempts to democratize still carry implicit messages about where power really lies: simply to attempt to switch power from

147

one group to another will not cancel the operation of power itself. The most honest approach is to acknowledge where the power lies at any one time.

This is not to say that the churches should not attempt to use or create spaces to allow other issues or other sections of the community to be given a hearing. However, this must be understood as an essentially ambiguous enterprise. There is perhaps a parallel here between Foucault's insights into the nature of power and Paul Tillich's view of the ambiguous nature of existence.[24] It is the latter's understanding of the mistake of trying to identify the kingdom of God with any political order which serves to save Christianity from being taken over by any one party programme. In the same way it is a mistake to identify Christian concepts of growth and maturity with any one model from the secular field. The Christian concepts can act as a constant critique because they are not meant to be so detailed. The specific programmes must always remain open to such critique because they are always subject to abuses of power and can become the means whereby one group or individual can attempt to coerce others. It is critical that this perspective on power should be kept in view, given the churches' growing involvement with the green movement which is, on one level, another political programme.

The acceptance of differences

The Christian tradition holds that in Christ each of us is unique. It is in God that the individual is offered a fearless space in which to appreciate others' differences. The sharing of personal stories within the life of the church is a way of acknowledging these differences. Relationships need space in which to grow, and the church can provide the deviant space in which this can happen, giving people confidence to rejoin the community. Most hurt and pain emerge in a social context, which therefore must also play an important part in restoring and healing. The environment of belonging provides the space in which to take risks. One of humanity's deepest fears is that of being left completely alone. Another is that one's life will be taken over by somebody else, so that the sense of uniqueness is diminished. The doctrine of the trinity holds together the unique work of each part of the Godhead in love. That symbol could help people to affirm their own uniqueness whilst feeling that they belonged to a wider community. It is the mystery of love that protects and respects the aloneness of the other and creates the free space where her loneliness can be converted into a solitude that can be shared. Each individual's story is unique and important, but often the individual becomes lost within the structure of the organization. What should be developed is a space to explore the unfolding tapestry of each member's life, for it is by the sharing of a personal story with others who will listen, that the sense of uniqueness and belonging will be fostered. We need ways of dealing with our history which give us a sense of continuity and personal identity. Early Methodism developed its class system to do just this and a strong 'society' was built up that was ready to go out into the wider community.

The church is a microcosm of our society with all its diversity. If there can be a recognition there that to be different does not pose a threat, then it can be used as a model for public life. The social life of the church is important in the context of the shared stories of its congregation, which give the opportunity to relate on a deeper level. If the future is to be rescued it will not be through magic or wishful thinking, but through the creation of a social structure which encourages us to take care of each other, and indeed of the whole of the natural world. People need a space where they can act lovingly. In fact, they cannot act at all unless they have a space in which to do so. If we come to see the damage we are inflicting we will have forced open around ourselves a moral space which gives room for action based on mutual vulnerability.

Community which bridges the gaps

The public place of the congregation could provide ways of relating to the local community. It could become a public place of hospitality where significant conversations can take place between friends and strangers. To enable the congregation to move from the norm of jumble sales and coffee mornings, to that of being active in and a redemptive influence upon society, demands a raising of confidence and an overcoming of low esteem so that those whose ideas are different are not viewed with suspicion, but find the campus open to them.

The word 'ecstasy' comes from two roots, 'ek' meaning 'out', and 'stasis' meaning 'standstill', in other words, to be outside a static place.[25] The complete joy we are promised as a gift leads to ecstatic living, that is, a willingness to leave the safe and secure and to reach out to others. Global ecstasy is a movement from fear to love; from living as rivals to living as people who belong to one community. The church has a divine calling, that of reconciliation. At a time when public life is all but invisible, it can help to create a public space in which people experience themselves as members of a community. Public life requires interaction with strangers. The church, with its vision of reaching out to those who are different, has a responsibility to act out this vision. It is up to the church to break the vicious circle of the public arena being a place of combat. It can offer a bridge from the private to the public by being the safe ground on which people can meet. So it is necessary for it to resist the temptation to become an extended family, because by doing that it would domesticate God, reducing him to a level we can cope with.

150

The church must stay open to strangeness, however uncomfortable that might be, and the Christian experience should protect pluralism by recognizing that many angles of vision are needed to see the whole. But it is often seen to want tightly-controlled relationships which deny God the opportunity to work. The message of Jesus is to live in the power of love in the midst of contradiction. The church is seen as the opposite of society, wanting comfort instead of conflict and intimacy rather than distance. Such a church can neither welcome the stranger, nor allow the stranger in each of us to emerge.

The stranger is a key figure in biblical stories because he takes the characters away from the safe and secure into the unknown. Everyday assumptions are shaken by the introduction of a stranger, and so people are able to hear God's word. We need the stranger if we are to know Christ and to live in faith, but to be comfortable with the external stranger we must be comfortable with the stranger within, as many divisions in the outer world are projections of divisions within the self. To avoid the stranger is to avoid being reminded of our isolation and so to create a world in which isolation deepens, this then being compounded by feelings of insecurity. To offer hospitality means to invite the stranger into a private space, a home, an awareness or concern, which then becomes an open space which can be illumined.

In the church, strangers can meet on common ground where fear is faced and dealt with, resources shared, conflicts owned and resolved, people drawn out of themselves and lives intertwined and given colour, texture and drama. People are empowered and protected against power, as a friendly emptiness is created where strangers discover themselves created free. It is a space which does not exist to modify, but rather to meet the individual's needs and enable them to grow. Hospitality can be extended to strangers, offering to host discussions between groups

151

in the community who are in conflict. Space is provided for its own members by letting God be the one who provides the hospitality, the one in whom gaps are bridged. Any meeting with a stranger will be seen as a chance to learn something new, if we allow God to be the third person in all our meetings. Then fear is replaced by hope. So the church can become a community which frees us from the insularity of private life and leads to a creative public life.

How, then, are Christians to understand their political involvement? One option is to make a conscious decision to stay out on the margins of political life. In other words, to be prepared to offer critical comments and suggestions about what is believed to be wrong, but to limit any discussion of positive alternatives. It is not our task to enter into the detailed debate of how a government should conduct the delicate process of negotiation required to achieve a reduction of greenhouse gases, for instance. The Christian role is to establish from within the tradition that the question of how to treat the natural world requires a moral dimension, and not merely a technical fix. The resources of language and space contribute to setting up that debate in the wider society, but without either pre-empting it by imposing Christian answers, or by selling out unthinkingly to the green movement. If this is deemed to be ineffective, or if credibility in the wider debate demands a more direct involvement in the political process, then there must be greater efforts to come to terms with the complexities of contemporary politics. To do less is to risk being appropriated by existing political power networks and becoming uncritically engaged with them.

We would like to propose one playful suggestion which may help to illustrate this. Let us call this 'The String Vest Theory'. For a string vest to be effective there has to be a certain amount of string. Too little and there is no vest. However, the warmth is trapped in the holes between the string. If there is too much string then there will not be enough warmth. The trick is to get the optimum balance between string and holes. All institutional life, including formal politics, is of this nature. There are those whose task is continually to adjust the string in order to alter the balance, but what really matters is what slips through the gaps. Perhaps Christians should concentrate their attention on working in those gaps, the non-institutional side of politics. This has a parallel in the theory of the relationship between the state and what is called civil society. Civil society is the sphere of the gaps between the formal structures of political life, operating in the spaces where there is greater freedom and a greater opportunity to express more radical thoughts and feelings. Leave the string to the politicians: perhaps this is where Christianity has the greatest contribution to make.

Conclusion

In conclusion we now suggest five areas where theology might learn from this discussion about creating spaces. First, it should acknowledge that this is a serious subject for study, given that it emerges from the fields of philosophy, sociology and politics. Second, Christianity should become more aware of its power over existing spaces, through buildings, meetings and language, and also of its capacity to create new spaces. Third, it should make more of an effort to establish a critical involvement with other movements concerned with the same moral issues. This would also include a comparison with their methods of operation. Fourth, there should be an understanding that there is no such thing as neutral space and that any spaces, old or new, are always already connected to networks of power and therefore essentially ambiguous. Fifth, the churches should seek to avoid the temptation of closing potential space down by jumping into debates with pre-determined answers.

It seems that Christianity has more to offer to the ecological debate than simply encouraging its youth groups to pick up litter, or its older members to patronise recycling programmes. There are four main areas where the church has something distinctive to say.

First, Christianity reminds us that we are 'pots of earthenware' (2 Corinthians 4.7), that we are not yet perfect, and that while we aim for perfection we also have to admit the shadow side, that which we would rather deny but have to honour because it makes us what we are. This allows for the possibility of change and trans-formation. We know that, by ourselves, it may be impossible to change, but that with God all things are possible. This change requires the acceptance of the possibility of conflict, both with others who will oppose this and with ourselves.

One result of this admission of present imperfection is that while we still hold on to ideas we believe to be true, we also have to acknowledge that we can see only part of the truth. John Wesley, in his sermon 'The Catholic Spirit' said:

> I can't imagine anyone holding an opinion they know to be wrong, so each of us must be sure that our opinions are right. On the other hand we can hardly suppose that all our opinions, taken together, can be right. Human knowledge is limited and it is inevitable that we make mistakes . . . All wise people should therefore allow others the same liberty of opinion which they claim for themselves.[26]

This suggests that we should be able to accept the reality of 'the Other', the stranger, in a space where this can be realized.

Second, the search in which Christians are engaged is that for reconciliation and harmony, culminating in a vision of ultimate perfection. This can be the basis for the critique of other ideologies, but avoids confusing the present with the future. What has to be recognized is the need for both wider vision and the local action which attempts to put it into practice. Christ's death and resurrection is a model that Christianity has for this process. While these are historical events, they also point to a future hope for creation and thus have a far greater significance.

Rudolf Otto's idea of the numinous has helped many to describe the sense of otherness experienced when encountering the reality of God, and this is the third distinctive contribution that Christianity can make.[27] This provides the distance for reflection which is necessary for any group or community to be able to see beyond themselves. This mystery is inevitably elusive, but if we lack some sense of otherness we tend to create our own mystery anyway.

The fourth idea is that of the campus, a place where differences can be aired but damage limited. The church can provide this space and within this, people can discover their gifts while being able to acknowledge that others also have a unique contribution to make. This view of the church does not correspond to the romantic image of a perfect family but allows for the possibility of conflict and disagreement. Differences can be honestly shared in a safe environment. Perhaps this is the most important role that the church can play in the ecological debate, providing a forum for open discussion.

These conclusions lead to criteria for a critique of much of the green theology. All publications should be faced with the following questions: Do they provide an open space for the conduct of debate and allow for genuine disagreement? Do they provide the basis for an ideology critique rather than just presenting the illusion of a simplistic harmony with nature and with others? Do they provide a search for a moral discourse which has direct political implications and which attempts to bridge the gap between private and public life? Finally, do they provide procedures for handling conflict while respecting differences? It is our contention that much of the current literature fails to meet these criteria.

Notes

1. For example, *Faith in the Countryside* (Churchman 1990), Jonathan Porritt, *Seeing Green* (Blackwell 1984), pp. 209–211.
2. Alberto Melucci, *Nomads of the Present* (Hutchinson Radius 1989), p. 56.
3. E. F. Schumacher, *Small is Beautiful* (Blond & Briggs 1973).
4. T. S. Eliot, *Murder in the Cathedral* (Faber & Faber 1935), p. 75.
5. Claus Offe, *Disorganized Capitalism* (Boston, Polity Press, 1985), p. 291.
6. John A. Sanford, *The Kingdom Within* (San Francisco, Harper and Row, 1987), p. 146.
7. Jim Cotter, *Prayers at Night* (Sheffield, Cairns Publications, 1988), p. 55.
8. Martin Heidegger, *Poetry, Language, Thought* (San Francisco, Harper and Row, 1971), p. 53.
9. John Reader, 'On a Methodology for Pastoral Theology', *Modern Churchman*, vol. 31, no. 1, 1990.
10. Jürgen Habermas, *The Structural Transformation of the Public Sphere* (Polity Press 1989).
11. Habermas, p. 55.
12. Habermas, p. 159.
13. Alain Touraine, *The Voice and the Eye* (Cambridge University Press 1978).
14. Melucci and Habermas, *The Theory of Communicative Action*, vol. 2 (Polity Press 1987), p. 391ff.
15. Melucci, p. 56.
16. John Reader, 'Local Theology and the New Social Movements – An Illuminating Affinity', *Modern Churchman*, vol. 23, no. 4, 1991.
17. Parker Palmer, *The Company of Strangers* (New York, Crossroad 1989).
18. Henri Nouwen, *In the House of the Lord* (Darton, Longman & Todd 1988), p. 38.

19. Salman Rushdie, 'Is Nothing Sacred?', Oxford and Southwell Institute for Church and Society Papers, Summer Issue 1989.
20. Thomas Merton, *Raids on the Unspeakable* (Burns & Oates 1966), p. 11.
21. Jürgen Moltmann, *Creating a Just Future* (SCM Press 1989), p. 81.
22. Michel Foucault, *Discipline and Punish - The Birth of the Prison* (Peregrine Books 1979). Also, *The Birth of the Clinic; An Archeaology of Medical Perception* (Tavistock 1973).
23. Michel Foucault, 'Afterword: How is Power Exercised?' in Hubert Dreyfus and Paul Rabinow, *Michel Foucault: Beyond Structuralism and Hermeneutics* (University of Chicago Press 1982).
24. Paul Tillich in *Systematic Theology*, vol. 2 (SCM Press 1978), p. 132.
25. Nouwen, p. 38.
26. John Wesley, *Sermons on Several Occasions*, rendered in modern English by James D. Holway (Derby, Moorleys, 1987), p. 393.
27. Rudolf Otto, *The Idea of the Holy* (Oxford University Press 1950), p. 68.

Three Approaches for Environmental Exploration

The church's response to environmental matters has been limited, and this is in part a structural problem. If churches are to explore any issues effectively then they cannot escape the implications expressed in the words of the jazz standard, 'There'll be some changes made'. But what's to be done? In the earlier review of the church's response we saw the need for people to be actively involved in creative processes, rather than just being the largely passive recipients of someone else's efforts. The action to be taken will largely depend on local circumstances. Some of this could be based on varieties of community action that assist in dealing directly with local issues, methods that assist people in a pluralistic society to articulate their concerns and develop appropriate ethical responses. We have chosen three examples that use a largely creative approach: pilgrimage, community drama and art. The first two are taken from direct and shared experience of working and experimenting at Bishop's Castle Community College in south west Shropshire. They are supplemented by Lindsay Brown's article on the use of art, her work occurring within the same community.

First it is necessary to briefly outline some of the implications of their use. Practice has shown that to be used effectively, pilgrimage, community drama and art require

considerable amounts of time and therefore imply considerable changes in established working practice. They are
also of some danger to other well-regulated situations,
such as school routines. However, we are engaged in
'adventures' and that requires explorations for appropriate
method. There is new ground to discover – or maybe to
rediscover. This exploration takes the church into developing
its whole-community function. There is no blueprint, no
simple solution. The key elements are flexibility both
theological and practical, and considerable use of creative
approaches. Recent developments in the theory of professional ministry (and of the role of the teacher in the
classroom) are useful pointers. They suggest 'enabling'. To
achieve an effective enabling process, those who are
instigating it need to maintain a wide view. They must try
and avoid being locked into a group 'language' (this is as
true for other professions as it is for church ministers). The
view is outward and the expectation is of change. Other
examples of method could have been introduced. But we
are working from our experience. Whilst the examples may
be of interest, and may prove to be useful, others may have
widely different, but equally effective, methods. Curiously,
despite all the foregoing discussion about the need for
radical change, the practices offered have ancient roots.
The whole of the Judaeo-Christian tradition is based on
journey, from the story of Adam and Eve's expulsion, to
Abram's journey, to the Exodus and through to medieval
times. Even the reformers could not ignore journey and
pilgrimage, with examples such as the Pilgrim Fathers,
Wesleyan sites and the recent Mormon experience.
Community art and drama come from traditions that
include tribal tale-telling, Sophocles and the medieval
mysteries, all providing occasions during which certain
ideas could be expressed that might not otherwise surface.

8

Pilgrimage

IAN BALL

Pilgrimage as an image has been described as 'the mirror of life', most notably in Bunyan's *The Pilgrim's Progress*. There have been varieties of pilgrimage; Ingrid Lukatis identified four basic types: of salvation; of penitence and expiation (including for others); of devotion; of commitment.[1]

In her article Lukatis comments, 'exaltation is no longer the result of a miraculous experience but of the experience of the whole journey'. This emphasis on the experiences of the journey rather than the goal is increasingly common[2] and is central in the Church of England report, 'Children in the Way'. The report attempted to find an appropriate method of working with young people and examined various 'models'. Its main suggestion was that a 'pilgrim church' model should be used: 'the pilgrim community comprises a band of people all sharing in and learning from common experience . . . united in reaching a common goal.'[3]

Now what sort of pilgrimage are they seeking? Does the image of pilgrimage in this report relate to any of the recognized types mentioned above? Unfortunately, as there is no analysis of pilgrimage or definition of what style of pilgrimage is being adopted, exactly what is intended is unclear. The report makes many valuable points about the way pilgrimage allows for what is today regarded as sound educational practice: 'intergenerational learning', 'learning . . . a life long process'.[4] Further, in the theological reflection, the manner in which the traditional scripture is used contrasts neatly with the manner of its use in the more recent ACORA report. Rather than relying on a specific passage, it deals with the general thrust of an idea found in the ancient texts that works in well with the modern approaches: 'What the pilgrim church needs to help it on its way are stories of the past to help map out the journey; common worship in which the living God is experienced; and a confidence in an unknown future.'[5] Good stuff, and not what traditional Christianity would have presented. But where is this pilgrimage going? We seem to be left to work out the answer for ourselves.

In the typology outlined by Lukatis, the 'goal' remains observable. Even in its most modern form, the 'pilgrimage of commitment' there is a recognizable aim. If we include examples such as the Aldermaston Marches or walks associated with Greenham Common, we are dealing with events that have particular, definable aims. But when we use pilgrimage as an appropriate image for our work with children, we have no clearly stated aim. The nearest to a stated aim that the report reaches is the chapter 'Growing in Faith'. In using Fowler's 'stages of faith' it cites 'the final stage . . . where coherence gives a new simplicity centred on "a oneness beyond but inclusive of the manyness of Being"!'.[6] Again, as with so much that is produced at present, there is in this work a tacit admission that the church is in a much more open situation than is often realized by most non-churchgoers. The language being used is open to all manner of interpretation. The failure to describe an aim to the pilgrimage in anything but the most general terms ('growing in faith') is another indicator of change.

The idea of pilgrimage works because as well as seeming to fit tradition, it offers change and risk. There is more adventure associated with the idea than with fixed models, and there is no need for rigid hierarchies: learning can be achieved by all. So, as an approach to work within the church, it has appeal, though a new style of pilgrimage is being developed. Alan Morinis states,

> The social function of pilgrimage has been seen to be of three types . . . (1) 'a force in national or regional social integration cutting across group boundaries'; (2) 'the institution functions to develop or maintain values and ideas held by the group'; (3) 'the replication of existing social patterns in pilgrimage practices . . . pilgrimage serves to reinforce existing patterns of social relations within the area from which the pilgrimage draws pilgrims'.[7]

It is interesting to set these views alongside those of Ingrid Lukatis. They illustrate the complex nature of pilgrimage. As we begin to consider how to use pilgrimage as an activity, it is as well to be aware of the types. The functions described by Morinis all reinforce existing attitudes and views, even if they are not those initially held by the pilgrims. The sort of pilgrimage that is needed for the present age is one in which exploration of new ways occurs – a pilgrimage of discovery. In some senses it will relate to Morinis's second function (and Lukatis's pilgrimage of commitment) because no one can come to anything without something. The interaction that occurs will therefore start from where people 'are'. But the intention is to discover new depth, and the group being brought together needs to recognize and rejoice in its diversity (and that achievement alone would be quite important).

Thus there is a new function for pilgrimage: pilgrimage as an agent for development and change. Whatever is planned and practised should attempt to provide for that. Gone are all attempts to inculcate some established external 'truth' that is considered by those who organize and control the event, to be of 'value' for the pilgrims. The need is for a pilgrimage that brings together the separateness, that creates togetherness, that develops for its own time, recognizing the value of the members and of those whom they touch as they process to their chosen goal. It needs to work against dissimulation. And the pilgrims become as 'strangers in the land', but having at least learned the intrinsic value of everything they encounter.

So what might a pilgrimage allow? I would suggest that the following are some of the issues that might be considered: community, friendship, mutuality, struggle, clarity, personal and group assessment, link with place, new visions, revisioning, responsibility, sharing, developing stories, breaking barriers, discovering worth, achievement, exercising inborn motility, bonding, developing common texts, charging aesthetic batteries, quiet moments, developing appropriate ritual, proper organization, accepting failure, followers and leaders, reading maps, ignoring maps, celebration, imaging, accepting the end, fearing the beginning, anticipation, tedium, hardship, release.

Whatever the issues and elements that might arise, the action of pilgrimage at least has potential for allowing space for the participants to explore matters that are of vital importance to them. These may not be on the official agenda, but the nature of a walking pilgrimage is such that they will at some point be likely to surface. If it is possible to allow this to happen (and that cannot be guaranteed), then people may begin to struggle with major issues together. And that that should occur matters. At this point the act of pilgrimage begins to catalyze the exploration of ethics and becomes a means of discovering a sense of 'the other'. Individualism and isolation are forcefully challenged.[8]

It is to be hoped that all the potential recognized in 'Children in the Way' will be realized. To perform a pilgrimage should be seen as an activity that is open to all. Too often 'adventures' are left to the energetic. Too often activities such as pilgrimages are presented as simply reinforcement exercises for the committed. Outsiders may be permitted but they have to tolerate moments of confessional activity, without being encouraged to add their own alternative contribution. One of the major complaints made by the objectors to the WWF Canterbury pilgrimages was that they allowed other faiths 'space' in a Christian setting. Now many confessing Christians would find the objectors' position distasteful, accepting that as we live in a multi-faith society some sharing of worship is not unreasonable. But received tradition underlies the logic of the objections: the objections are well grounded on an exclusivist past. Such a position needs now to be firmly rejected. But we should realize that if we do that we are accepting the principle of change. Therefore, if we are able to accept change to allow space for those who have different religious faiths, then why stop there? It really is time that those in positions of authority in the church stated more boldly their acceptance of the implications of modern thought.

I now intend to discuss some of the elements required for a pilgrimage. These elements create the dynamic. A pilgrimage in the traditional mode, with its aim of reinforcing or recharging faith, will contain most of them. The difference with a pilgrimage that is intentionally 'open' in concept is that the process of the activity is more important than the chosen destination – 'the medium is the message', if one listens.

A group planning any such event needs to consider its purpose, and engage in detailed planning. It may be that there will be a significant goal, which may be a traditional pilgrimage site. It may be that there is a theme; sponsored walks function in this manner. It could be that the pilgrimage is associated with community boundaries after the fashion of Rogationtide perambulations, or occurs at a significant time such as Holy Week. Ideally there should be a chosen goal of some significance (for it will by its nature provide some quality to the activity), and a group that has chosen to walk there. There are many roles that though seemingly 'only' supportive (such as driving a support vehicle) are essential and allow, ultimately, for many participants to share the start and finish. Too often when such activities occur, they are seen as 'for the young', and they are also viewed as only for those interested. It may be that for practical reasons the group of walkers is only small, but attempts should be made to involve as many as possible. The preparations should be as creative as possible and ideally should allow for detailed discussion and consultation with all those involved. It is easy to imagine a group preparing for this event week by week and exploring the theme of journey, or the theme that the journey takes, in a host of ways. The group should if possible be drawn from a wide cross-section of whatever community it is coming from. Thus if it is an established church group the activities may be reasonably confessional (though hopefully they would be experimental). However, it is to be hoped that the group sharing the pilgrimage will be required to be accepting of all views and attitudes.

The journey itself, ideally lasting for five days at least, will help bring barriers down. It will function in the fashion of a reasonably rigorous retreat. Accommodation should be a series of village or church halls (non-walking supporters may cast themselves on the mercy of the local populace or even be permitted the luxury of an inn!), with the food prepared by the group. Those used to expeditions of various sorts will be well aware how revealing of character are such occasions. They will also be aware of the strains and difficulties that small but persistent privations create.[9] It may be argued that it is impossible to expect people to give five days (or more) to participating in such an event. It is largely a question of priorities, and that applies to all the suggestions that this book is making. We will always find reasons for not doing things, even after they have been shown to be important. That particular problem is one of the greatest facing those involved with teaching environmental issues.

We all need to create space in order to assess priorities. How do established church groups do that at present? Whilst suggesting that pilgrimage allows for 'space' I have to recognize from years of experience that one of the greatest messages coming from a walking pilgrimage is that there is no time for anything else but performing the pilgrimage. Even in the best of weather, the business of putting one foot in front of the other, for several days on end, is all that can really be expected. The times when one is relieved from doing that is simply best spent in the pub. These places are themselves a potential space in which people may exchange in various ways, and significantly, unlike the structured activities associated with a church building, groups meeting in them are often able to set their own agendas.

Some groups may wish for more than just the evening collapse, the empty time which is filled by chance meeting or personal retreat. Much depends on the planning, but also on the deep awareness of what the group might achieve. If there are to be evening activities (or extras fitted in during the day) then the length of the day's walk needs to be considered. Whatever is decided, it should always be regarded as important that all efforts are made to allow everybody who starts to finish. Different people have different levels of endurance.

A well prepared pilgrimage could contain other elements that may help establish a sense of purpose for the journey and develop links with those one meets, such as a simple improvised dramatic production, or a travelling art exhibition. Organizing such things is not as difficult as may at first seem. Effective work on these lines is probably best left until the event itself, and then it can never be guaranteed. Too much preparation can stifle the opportuni-

167

ties produced by chance, and may also produce an excessive cocoon effect.

Does one community wish to share with other communities? And what are the boundary limits that any community sets? Is it just church group talking to church group, or could it just be that the church group in any one place acts to draw others into the event and allows them space to share? Here is the test of faith. The church has the network and can act as a focus for resources, but must it always control the agenda? If it is acting according to John Reader's 'String Vest' theory, surely it must primarily be an enabling institution, allowing as many as possible to come together to work out together what matters. 'What matters' may be essentially local, but can also be wider. Whatever the 'what matters' is, the result will be the development of ethics.

Now all this may give the impression that careful preparation produces the required result. This, of course is not so. One of the delights of performing a pilgrimage is its unpredictability. People fail. Those who set out to walk to a destination which is several days' journey away wish, not surprisingly, to reach it, but they may not be able to. Even for experienced adults failure is hard to take.

The major question as we turn to the theme of this book is, 'How does this relate to a response to environmental matters?' In answering that it becomes necessary to discuss the matter of relationships in general; until we have a reasonable relationship with other humans we are unlikely to develop much of a concern for other life-forms (never mind the inanimate world). The present state of Eastern Europe illustrates that the repression of people was being paralleled by a dreadful neglect for aspects of the natural world.[10] Our environmental improvements are often related to human need as much as to the separate needs of other species. That may be an attitude that needs to be changed, but it is at present the way things are. A concern for human relationships is vital. Now if it is possible to see that Christianity in its broadest sense has articulated that concern, then it has a major contribution to make. As the vision of improving relationships is approached, other wider issues will become clearer.

A successful pilgrimage will have 'encountered' the issue of relationships, even if it is part of the hidden agenda. For a pilgrimage that is openly environmental in its concerns, the 'encounter' should be public, in that, in the preparations or on the walk itself, it should be within the 'dialogue'. Dialogue can involve a variety of methods: drama, art, music, as well as discussion. But if we are to include 'relationships' in the dialogue, a concern for relationships must be in the structure of the event, for we are known by our deeds. 'Who does what and why?' is a vitally important question. The pilgrimages being envisaged here are not 'expert led nature rambles', they are for all those involved to share. So leadership structure matters and should allow for participation (or not, as the individual members wish). There needs to be some form of forum, and some form of democracy. One of the greatest mistakes that I have made as an organizer was to provide a rigid leadership structure on a pilgrimage which involved people with varied tastes and interests. Consequently there developed a jostling for position. Some of the participants had strong views that they wished to represent to others, but there was no official means of so doing. Consequently there was friction between members of the group. There was a degree of resolution before the end caused by the 'bubble factor'. We were a group, whatever our differences, travelling together, our own little 'lifeworld', separate from everything that we passed, strangers to all we met, and therefore inevitably bonded to one another. Arrivals demonstrate the degree of separateness one has had from daily existence, and in this case, as in many others, some of those who found the relationships most demanding were the ones who clung

169

most carefully to what had been created during the walk. However, the whole event might have been more satisfying for everyone if it had included daily meetings.

There is a tendency with pilgrimages involving adolescents to lead without consultation. Kids are used to being led and teachers expect to do it, though that is no excuse for continuing the pattern. Here the church can act in a much more effective manner than the formal education system. It creates the relationship pattern that it chooses. It does not need to fit in with an existing system (though the authoritarian model is sadly normal). Thus it could easily operate 'democratic management' even with younger groups. If it wishes to assist in the 'growth' of those whom it is assisting then it should not make assumptions about their belief positions. Democratic management extends to every aspect of the activity and responsibilities have to be agreed by the group.

After structural matters there are other ways in which a pilgrimage can serve to stimulate interest and debate on matters environmental. The WWF pilgrimages to Canterbury, in their publicity material, outlined a valuable, open approach: 'The meaning of this pilgrimage to Canterbury is to bring together environmentalists and non-environmentalists, believers and non-believers, giving them a chance to share emotions, ideas and stories from their own cultures and ways of life in search of a common understanding to establish strong and lasting human links'. This level of activity can be achieved if the basics are right, namely, proper preparation (equipment, catering, etc), appropriate structure, appropriate goal, route and mileages.

Many people involved in 'green' issues are realizing that simply choosing the greenest product is not all that is required. A much deeper, structural change is necessary. Our present approaches that unconcernedly require us to 'take what we can' from each situation, need to be changed.

Our relationships with each other and with the rest of creation are in need of improvement. The underlying message of the WWF's stated approach to the pilgrimage is that without openness shown by each to the other, nothing will change.

Simply walking through the land exposes us to openly environmental matters. It places us back on our original human scale of size, speed and dependence. It should not be imagined that we can in any way recapture what it felt to be mediaeval, but it is quite humbling (and exciting) to stand on a hill looking over the countryside and see distant hills that are 'four days' journey hence'. If one is pained by blisters, a heavy pack and cheerily successful companions, such a sight raises other feelings as well!

As well as assisting with the business of restoring a sense of proportion, walking through a landscape gives one a deeper than normal sense of human interaction with it. Therefore it is worth attempting to construct a route that is not simply picturesque, but that provides a variety of experiences of land use including suburban and industrial. One fascinating pilgrimage included the Potteries with chance meetings with ex-pottery employees, and consequent insights into traditional working practices. Later in the same walk, having experienced the white hares of the remoter reaches of the Peak District, we viewed the rhubarb fields (or what is left of them) in industrial West Yorkshire. Likewise on another walk, we experienced twenty miles of strength-sapping flatness crossing the agri-businessed Fens near Ely, whilst being bombarded by lightning and torrential rain. Then a day later we passed by the eerie privacy of an RAF base near Castle Acre producing a very different, but more deeply worrying, mysterious thunder. On another walk, we discovered the basic poverty of Surrey – the thin soils that left it neglected until the last century. Thus it is possible to

171

gain a sense of people, place and time, and to consider where we now are and where we might be: 'Remembering the Future'.[11]

Part of the charm of pilgrimage is that it leaves the security of everyday normality. It involves movement out and away. But there is always a return at the end of the pilgrimage, a return to the daily pattern. The work that Richard Beaumond is presenting covers much of the same ground, but without departure from home. However, if followed in detail, home is never again the same place that it was before The Drama. A whirlpool is created, the bottom of which is always unseen until the end. Pilgrimages can be more terrifying than some people realize. They can be great promenade performances in which the participants are both actors and spectators. The landscape changes.

And community drama? It can be a great promenade performance in which the participants are both actors and spectators. The landscape never changes, but is never the same again. And is all this just wishful thinking? A series of nice ideas? 'All very well on paper, but no such thing in the field'? That will be said. But the church is diverse and complex. There will always be places where some form of sanctuary is offered from the frightening noise of the modern world, but in those places there is little hope of real encounter or assistance in adjusting to modernity and, in the process, adjusting it. However there are already places in which, in various ways, the struggle to adjust is occurring. In time we all pass on and the strangers of the future will puzzle over our stupidity. But as for now, as the Cajun dance tune says: 'Bon ton roulez' . . .[12]

Notes

1. Ingrid Lukatis, 'Church Meeting and Pilgrimage in Germany', *Social Compass* (Sage Publications) June 1989, p. 204. Interestingly, the

article is about the Protestant Kirchentag, which in itself is a fine example of the manner in which the church can create open-space into which a wide variety of views can be put. Quoting the founder of the movement (Thadden-Trieglaff), Lukatis writes: 'As a Protestant lay movement, the Church Meeting was "to give the church lay help that she might break the bounds of the ghetto in which she had too long permitted herself to be imprisoned, might open the gates wide to the world and assume her thoroughly modern mission"'.

2. For example, 'Pilgrimage is not simply about places but about people . . . encountering others and interacting with them.' J. G. Davies, *Pilgrimage Yesterday and Today* (SCM Press), p. 204. And: 'There is benefit in pilgrimage if checked by a theology of the presence of God and of his activity in his world. The consequence would be greater emphasis on the journey, with less on the destination.' Christopher Lewis, 'On going to Sacred Places', *Theology*, September 1989.

3. 'Children in the Way', A Report from the General Synod Board of Education (National Society/Church House Publishing), p. 33.

4. 'Children in the Way', p. 33.

5. 'Children in the Way', p. 77.

6. 'Children in the Way', p. 53.

7. Morinis, *Pilgrimage in the Hindu Tradition* (Oxford University Press, Delhi, 1984), p. 238ff.

8. On a personal level, I recall the effect of being 'on pilgrimage' during the build-up to the Falklands conflict and the formative impact of the general conversation on the views of many of us. Such memories are prompted in the wake of the Gulf War at a time when the full (and predicted) effect of the conflict is beginning to be felt. Do we all sit at home and allow the professional media to fix our opinions, or can we find some place in which we are at leisure to explore our feelings and concerns? The question that the church must always be asking itself is, 'Are we assisting people in their struggle for meaning?'

9. This element should not be underestimated in planning. Most of us, for most of the time, lead very comfortable lives. The idea of walking for days has a romantic appeal that often covers the harsh realities. Some of my students believe that 'it's not a proper pilgrimage until he's lost his temper' . . . That comment was made late at night in Walsingham!

10. The spoilation of the waters of the Gulf and the likelihood of widespread and damaging acid rain from the oil fires, are other

good examples. It is worth considering how much of this problem is related not simply to Saddam Hussein's dictatorship, but also to the requirement on the part of the USA for a successful war. However the situation is viewed, our concern for human issues overrode our concern for other non-human concerns.

11. 'To hope is to remember the future' – George Steiner. Part of 'Remembering the Future', an address given at King's College, London, and reprinted in *Theology*, November 1990.

12. 'Let the good times roll'.

9

Community Drama

RICHARD BEAUMOND

The essence of the environmental situation is that traditional links with the land which held good for centuries have, in a matter of decades, disappeared. This is largely due to the rush of twentieth century technology which created a situation of global communication coupled with personal isolation. A recent illustration of this is the early 80's love affair with CB radio – an eminently sensible and useful means of contact in an area the size of America. In England, however, users adopted the argot of the Americans and shivered in cold cars talking in crazy codes to people they would brush past in the street without a nod of acknowledgement, let alone a word.

In the Britain of the early years of this century, the links with the land were clear: communities lived and worked together, limited (as Laurie Lee noted) by the horizon of their valley or the distance they could walk in a day. Life, and the seasons with their tasks and associated social rituals, nurtured a mutual respect and dependency between the land and its people which was recognized by society and reinforced by tradition which everyone – including the churches – acknowledged and used to their advantage.

The means of social contact were bound in with the way of life: walking to work or school, sowing and reaping, gleaning; the rabbit warren as communal larder, the communal rights to gather firewood and cut turf, the care of the heavy horse on which so much rested, and the sharing of plenty.

In rural England this communality disappeared with the Great War and the coming of the internal combustion engine. Both events may be regretted, inflicted as they were on a helpless population by the rich and privileged. As it became possible to live in one place, work in another and socialize somewhere else the link between community and land disappeared.

By the mid 50s orchards were becoming lawns for retired people who sought little outside contact. These lawns became the building plots for unaesthetic dwellings for yet more incomers whose presence destroyed that peace which they sought to share. In urban areas the notion of the inner city village did not survive the second war, despite the myth propagated by inner-city soap operas like 'EastEnders' at one end and suburban soaps like 'Brookside' at the other.

For many people, isolation is actually what they want, and they foster the division between the new and the old villagers, now herded onto council estates on the fringes. That section of the population that lives, works and socializes in the same place is even more marginalized and no longer expresses the caring relationship with the land through its work.

This is no plea for halcyon days. I well remember dank houses, dark lanes, racking coughs and sad, drawn faces in the dismal procession to the church. We need the light and warmth and contact. We need to replace some of the old, redundant links with new networks, to foster again the sense of the broad church; the linking of the land with its people. Hereafter, I am suggesting that community arts activity provides ways of doing that; looking at the present, through the past, to the future, and providing a means of joining a debate in which we can no longer afford not to take part.

As we approach the new millennium, extreme examples of the rootlessness of populations, and the environmental and social consequences of rapid or declining development are of increasing concern and need to be approached on many levels: international, national and local. Imposed solutions from governmental or extra-governmental levels do not have a good history: at a very local level we can enable and empower people to question and draw conclusions, to criticize and celebrate, to raise consciousness, develop awareness and perhaps to gain the little bit of confidence necessary to reach out a hand; renew some old links and create new ones appropriate to the times and circumstances in which we live.

Community Drama

What causes me to advocate community arts activity of one sort or another? It is simply a belief that people, on the whole, are the better for company, and that life is ultimately more satisfying if parts of it are shared. It should go almost without saying that art is for everybody, that everybody should, as a matter of right, have access to arts, skills and experience. The arts of which I am writing is a very broad church indeed, accessible in very general terms but capable of application in terms of a range of very specific skills. A church which is non-creative is hardly representative of the 'Gospel'. This section of the book is intended to start the reader thinking about practical activity that is of value to the environmental debate and the church's role in it.

Projects always begin in the mind and transfer to the ground through a greater or lesser mound of paper. The resultant product and experience may be very different from the initial mental picture, but that should not in any way mean it is less satisfying or a diminished experience.

Part of the importance of community projects, and especially community drama, is the raising and articulating of issues that affect the functioning and development of a community; effecting a dialogue that may at least raise issues and consciousness and at best might cause the solving of problems.

There are no guaranteed models of success that will superimpose from one community to another, but there are common factors: people – this is who it is for and what it is about; their environment – physical, social and spiritual; the need to articulate issues and feelings; the desire to feel for conclusions and make statements about the individual and community; developing a sense of place in time and space; art (and drama) as an enabling and empowering agent to effect change; the capacity to enrich communities beyond the limits of the artistic experience itself.

Community arts projects, and especially community drama, are a powerful experience having considerable emotional effect. Relationships will form and fracture in the intensity of the experience – it always happens. It is not necessarily possible to be your brother's keeper, but there are plainly instances where responsibility must be assumed for the physical safety and emotional well-being of, for example, youth and children involved.

The pressure of the experience of the production process is considerable and will certainly test the level of commitment. For the core group, this needs to be total for the duration of the project. Other groups may be able to function as and when necessary. In the case of a community drama this might, for example, include the following situations: research group hands over to writing team; technical group is inactive until final rehearsals; construction team completes work before final rehearsals; backstage crew is inactive until move into performance space; research group takes on publicity. There are many variations and opportunities for people to contribute in more than one area.

Expert and informed opinion

It is necessary to refer to the use and availability of expert and informed opinion. Unless completely self-sufficient, an expert in your subject area, in control of your art form and utterly certain of your community, you are going to need the expertise and advice of professionals. Their services may be given free or bought in. As a matter of principle, you ought to pay professionals for what they do. This is an area where regional arts boards and local education authorities often have practical schemes in operation into which you can tap.

Even if you feel able to progress without professional help, it is a good idea to locate someone with appropriate skills and experience (a local community arts worker or a drama teacher, for example) to act as project adviser and later, evaluator; someone able to troubleshoot the process, to back up organization of the product and be prepared to give written and verbal evaluation afterwards; someone, if necessary, to act as a referee. Such a person might ensure that opportunities are created for everyone to voice opinion and concern; to take on broad ideas which will develop as involvement deepens, and to field criticism.

Even negative experiences can have positive learning values: 'I won't do that again!'

Process and product

The process is actually more important than the product. This in no way diminishes the responsibility for ensuring that the final product is the best, under the prevailing circumstances, of which you are capable.

179

It follows that any project must take risks and be prepared to fail. There can be few real guarantees of success, and anyway, who judges? Today's audience will have one perception, tomorrow's audience another. A performer has different feelings, and a funder other expectations ('I gave you money, therefore you must do so and so' is a difficulty which bedevils experiment and innovation at all levels).

For you, for the participants and for the community, the process is the product which goes beyond the final event of the project: enhanced community identity and self-image. This is why you must be sure of what you are doing, why you are doing it and who for. The 'how' of doing it is where the experimentation comes in.

Reflection is important as a means of evaluation. A basic opportunity occurs in natural breaks or after rehearsals: the work has shown a process of sharing and there should be room for a sharing of company, time, food, drink and enjoyment. This is a very important part of the process where space can be created that it is almost impossible to recreate in a manner of informal togetherness after the project. It is where some of the most important social and communal advances can be made. At the same time, retain awareness of the tendency to substitute talk for work.

The whole group should make an effort to celebrate little successes and milestones along the way; it is a road trodden together and the promenade includes the whole process, not just the performance. Afterwards, there should be a party, a celebration, a send-off, a wake, a release! It is not just the project but the whole process which one hopes will have positive effects beyond the time of the project itself. The whole process, not just the end-product performance, exhibition or publication should be thought of as an holistic experience: a pilgrimage or promenade through a period of community development.

Practical examples

Celebration

This can be centred on a local event. Every community can find something worth celebrating: research and sharing ideas can be the first step!

The celebration can involve a variety of art forms, events and opportunities for involvement. Events in local history and anniversaries provide the inspiration in many instances. For example, in 1887 Lydbury North celebrated Victoria's jubilee with an enormous procession through the village to Walcot Hall where over a thousand were wined and dined before taking part in children's games and country sports, picnic tea and country dancing.

This sort of scale may not be practical but enough could be done to give a flavour of the original events. It links celebration with local context, procession, dance and music. There are, of course, existing seasonal events and celebrations that might provide starting points.

Rural rides or town trails

These have practical applications and might involve school children working on what might become a parish council publication. There are clear links with the local environment, community and oral history projects. Consulting people with local knowledge might be the first step, then researching into particular locations and sites to establish a route and then finding the most suitable form of presentation. This could link with an event, such as beating the bounds. As well as a printed trail, an audio cassette could be produced.

Drama

Drama is often a way of presenting issues in a way that can be stimulating, thought-provoking and entertaining, at the same time as presenting material that is contentious and unacceptable in written form.

First, decide on your subject matter – old age, for instance. Research might include oral history plus tape/slide work with elderly people. Then create your story line illustrating the issues – disabilities, loneliness, illness, state provision, attitude of families, etc. Tour it to local schools, residential homes and village halls. Use it to open discussion and dialogue.

Community play

This can be done on either a grand or a localized scale. Of all the art forms that might be employed in community development, this is the one that has perhaps the greatest potential for involvement of very large numbers.

Music

Every community has musicians. You might provide a showcase for local talent – in aid of a local good cause – or base it around a theme; or it can be targeted specifically to suit particular tastes: junior discos, folk nights, jazz nights, blues nights, etc.

Scrap-book

Perhaps undertaken by a school group or residential group, a scrap-book might be compiled over a period of time from published sources, illustrated by personal photography or art and containing personal writing. Art therapists might be willing to contribute advice and help.

Book

This might develop from the scrap-book and involve oral history and photography on a given theme. There are many examples of this type of publication and many people who could give advice.

Sculpture

This can be permanent or semi-permanent, composed of a variety of materials, capable of being worked on by many people over a long period of time.

The Icarus Rising sculpture in the grounds of the Community College, Bishop's Castle, Shropshire is a case in point. The intention was to create a community sculpture based on the Icarus legend. It needed to be large, external and provide opportunities for practical involvement for many people of all ages, and related activities in music, dance and drama for many others.

The Community College was able to provide a site and undertake the administrative arrangements, including the raising of funds. This is not the place to go into detail but the act of fundraising, successful or otherwise, can be turned to advantage in terms of publicity, local involvement, creation of interest and raising awareness and the profile of the project. Beat the drums loud and long: even if you don't get the money, you get the interest and potential involvement. Small amounts make things possible and the goodwill engendered is often of great value in a small community. Various launch and publicity events were contrived and in the end over forty groups, businesses and individuals had contributed and were present at the opening ceremony which received considerable press attention and was an enjoyable occasion in itself.

The project period itself was just over three weeks of glorious autumnal weather. The period of preparation had

183

'ICARUS RISING'   *Martin Britnell*

184

been over a year and it is worth saying that the success and smooth running of the project is dependent on the quality of the preparation, though it is vital that space be left for the opportunities that cannot be foreseen but that will occur, and for the project to develop in ways that could not have been anticipated or planned for, but which are often most valuable.

The timber came from local barns of the medieval period: oak from trees that were young long before Drake was a lad, that gave a sense of place and a sense of history. Tools that go back with the land: chisels, axes and adzes that our grandparents used; not in themselves dissimilar to those used for generations before that. The older participants contributed skills and tales of work from their youth and rediscovered the pleasure of working with wood that the children were discovering for the first time.

Some people worked on the project throughout; others came in groups from secondary school, junior schools, play groups, residential homes for the elderly and the handicapped; some were very young and others were over eighty.

As the sculpture emerged – a skeletal prow of an ancient vessel orientated towards the iron age fort of Bury Ditches – under the chisels and axes of a multitude of hands, others worked on two labyrinths; twisted pottery figures rose through the maze and a new range of art forms, skills and techniques was employed.

Many people committed their thoughts, feelings and aspirations (inspired by the image of Icarus rising to the sun) to paper. These were placed in a time capsule and hoisted to the top of the mast, later to be buried beneath the sculpture. This was part of the opening ceremony.

Music was created and played for the occasion and a dance-drama took place in which Icarus rose, flew and fell to earth. Food and drink were shared and the performance became a social occasion. Throughout the afternoon and evening a steady stream of visitors passed through to look, feel, touch and climb over the sculpture for it has that quality, a real connection with the site, the locality and the people.

Stone work was added; two boys carved Icarus reaching for the sun on a four-foot slab of stone they lugged in themselves and the gardening club landscaped and planted the site. In spring and early summer it is floated on a sea of daffodils and two carved oaken figures nurse their child under the spreading branches of an oak tree as their ancient ark sails off into the future.

It still develops: a CND symbol has appeared, as well as one or two other motifs; occasionally tokens are hung on it – an echo of a very ancient custom – and often children sit on it.

There is every possibility that it will develop further and provide more opportunities for the expression of the community.

Environmental projects

An example of an environmental project would be the Community College's 'Bees and Trees' programme. This project grew out of a discerned need to provide a focus and expression for concerns about the environment on a very local scale but as part of a national movement.

The environmental agency 'Common Ground' had raised concern over the decline of old apple and fruit orchards and had toured an exhibition throughout the West Country. From this the Community College focused on the idea of a celebration of fruit orchards through craft, art and community activity: 'This celebratory weekend is a reaffirmation of the traditional links between the people and the land, symbolised by the tree, the apple and the bee.'

The planning involved many people in local communities

with interests in fruit, trees, bees, art, music, drama, conservation, gardening, education and social activity. Again, an autumnal weekend seemed appropriate: warm days and golden evenings with a low sun before the clocks change and thoughts turn towards the internal activities around the fireside.

Publicity, as ever, is the key, and an opening ceremony attracted a large crowd to see the Archdeacon of Ludlow plant three local fruit tree varieties in the college grounds. Displays remained open throughout the weekend and included exhibitions of two fruit tree planting projects in Ludlow and the Clun Valley involving children and their families; a display of identification processes for the many local apples that remain in the area but are now unknown; exhibitions of work on the Bees and Trees theme by local artists and craftspersons; observation hives and honey production processes; and a philatelic display of Bee and Tree theme stamps.

During the afternoon of the first day activities moved to Walcot Hall, Lydbury North, where a large and important arboretum had been planted towards the end of Victoria's reign. A local dendrologist led a guided tour and another expert described the work of restoration in the orchard.

This was followed by a 'bring and share' apple tea and picnic. There was a performance of the musical 'Johnny Appleseed' which is about the spread of English apple trees throughout the American west by one man who transported trees, seed and stocks across the Atlantic: an appropriate theme! Social activity in the evening centred on a country dance. Beverages included organic cider made from traditional cider apples.

The following day saw demonstrations and lectures on orchard and bee management – phrases currently much in vogue, and meaning the good practice that our grandfathers' generation would have expected. Grafting, pruning and skep-making were all on display. Later the prizes were

187

awarded for various produce: apples, honeys, waxes and pies.

Finally, in the evening the college hosted an ecumenical service in aid of the Shropshire Hospice Appeal, providing a good example of ways in which different sections of the community can come together to mutual advantage.

Six months later some of the work is still going on and two short poetry residencies are in the planning stage. Both have an environmental theme designed to touch the experience of the participants and the landscaping of a local factory site is to include the planting of fruit trees: community activity can actually influence events!

Fundamental to the success of any project is the perception of the scale on which it needs to operate. It is no use conceiving of an idea the community cannot accommodate. Nor is everything dependent on funding and circumstance. Everything is possible, but it is generally necessary to keep a practical eye on what can actually be achieved to avoid disappointment.

Bees and Trees and the Icarus Project also illustrate a truth that needs to be understood: there is little point in replicating something that has been done elsewhere, or putting a lot of effort into watered-down theatrical or musical experiences that belong elsewhere. The activity – whatever it is – needs local roots and resonance to give it life. A little research will expose all sorts of possibilities in the history and geography of an area, and the oral history of its people will provide even more.

Similarly lack of resources in terms of a theatre or hall need not be a stumbling block. Neither Bees and Trees nor Icarus needed much in the way of specialist venues and many projects can be sited in their natural settings.

Catalysts and Stimuli

Underlying this chapter is an assumption of arts-based

activity being a generally good thing in community work and life itself. Of course, some aspects will be more or less popular and drift in and out of fashion with greater or less acceptance.

From time to time circumstances occur in which it is possible to stimulate and initiate activity. For this writer, with a background of years of drama work in a variety of situations, the impetus over the last few years has come from the establishment of the Community College at Bishop's Castle in Shropshire.

In an area as remote, wide, sparsely-populated and covered with small and disparate communities as this part of the Welsh border, initiatives tend to be swallowed up by distances, lack of transport, poor publicity and cost. All over the area, which includes parts of Wales, village schools were putting out the lights at four o' clock in the afternoon and shutting down until the following day. The local secondary school at Bishop's Castle had a history of after-hours use by a couple of evening classes and the local amateur drama group on an occasional basis, but it was there as a resource and needed only a bit of commitment to get it open and used for a wide variety of activities. Evening transport was arranged and its embryonic arts programme was developed into a full year of music, art, drama, residencies and activities. It became host to all sorts of meetings, conferences on housing and the environment, school governor training, community development, church synod meetings, circle dancing, alternative health groups and all the other groups and societies that society forms itself into from time to time. Adults began to attend daytime classes with school pupils, courses from further education began to be sited there and it became a regular venue for touring theatre, musical concerts and lectures. All sorts of societies grew up and its newsletter became a magazine called 'Rabbit'. Now in its fourth year it grows and develops all the time.

The strength of the link between the people and the land, the environment and the community, and the development of a sense of identity, expressed through the arts: that is what community arts and drama is about. It really is for everyone – a means whereby communities can consider, and make statements about, the quality of their existence. In so doing they are enabled to enhance the very quality of that existence, that personal pilgrimage, the promenade through life itself.

10

Towards Synthesis – A Creative Approach

LINDSAY BROWN

Now, in this final chapter, we must ask ourselves, 'What does all this mean to *me*?' I would like to portray a way of relating, both to ourselves and in community, with particular reference to the points raised by John Reader and Margaret Goodall in their chapter, 'Creating Spaces'.

My approach is experiential, an attempt to balance thinking and feeling through the communion of creativity, specifically through the use of colour and symbol.

It springs from knowing that at the end of all our words the only raw material we have is each of us ourselves, in all our frailty and mystery; that sharing our strengths and vulnerability offers growth, and from growth comes response and service; and that the source of inspiration and energy come from the mystery both within and without, permeating all things. And which I call God.

What do we do about ourselves? Any ideas or theories first of all have to be related to ourselves. 'Sounds good! But how does it *feel*? What does it mean to me?'

The church has played a substantial part in suppressing any serious examination of self. By encouraging dependency for all spiritual and moral decision-making on the ecclesiastical hierarchy, it undermined people's desire or ability to take individual responsibility for their own lives.

The Christian ethic also actively discouraged introspection and any concept of self-exploration:

> In the past a moral conversion, a simple, whole-hearted devotion to a teacher or saviour, a loving surrender to God, were often sufficient to open the gates leading to a higher level of consciousness and a sense of inner union and fulfilment. Now, however, the more varied and conflicting aspects of modern man's personality are involved and need to be transmuted and harmonized with each other: his fundamental drives, his emotions and feelings, his creative imagination, his enquiring mind, his assertive will, and also his interpersonal and social relations.[1]

As we strive to find a new balance, there is a danger, perhaps born of fear and desperation, of swinging too far the other way from 'swallow the lot and you'll be OK' to thinking that all answers come from within. This denies the wider mystery, leaving little space for the stranger to enter. 'Working on ourselves' is the wounded healer theme,[2] yet without an honest commitment to face our fallibility, our fear, our wounds, to struggle towards self-knowledge and awareness, we cannot fully develop a wise and caring concern for community and environment. Through daring to own our weakness, we discover our strength.

Towards integration

It could be said that I have reduced this discussion to a merely personal perspective. And that is exactly what I am doing. From all the wide-ranging discourse and synthesis of ideas, through Ian Ball's and Richard Beaumond's dealing in community, I bring it down to the personal: myself, confronting myself.

This confrontation is not an isolated turning inward, but a process – often painful, sometimes joyful – of personal healing leading naturally into social action, service and the experience of vocation. Personal meaning cannot be separated from the meaning of one's life within a larger scheme of things. The inner journey of self-exploration, discovery and expression is more connected to the needs of humanity and the planet than to self-gratification. It is personal, yet greater than the self.

It is through this struggle that we become aware of our capacity for good, as well as our capacity for evil; to live without self-deception or self-illusion is to continually ascend and descend the ladder between good and evil, heaven and hell. 'Man, know thyself' is a lifelong quest.

How we live our lives can only reflect this inner state of truth and healing. True healing demands change. It demands courage, vision, vulnerability, perseverance, fluidity, humility, imagination, will, risk, acceptance, interdependence, struggle, pain, resources, support, companionship, letting go, understanding, love, and recognition of ultimate mystery (whether one calls that God or not).

How willing are we to open and make ourselves vulnerable? How willing are we to be healed?

A possible way

How do we find and use a language which both exposes and connects us to our deeper selves and relates us to others and the wider community?

Jung believed that art represents a new synthesis between the inner subjective world of the artist and external reality. The artist has at all times been the spokesman for the spirit of his age, and historically art and religion have always been intertwined.

It seems to me that as the church, at least from the fourth century on, assumed a hierarchy, so we have allowed artistic expression an élitist position – something 'taken care of' by those involved in 'the arts'. Until the church began losing power to state and government, it had been the main patron of the arts. The subject matter was confined almost exclusively to allegory and biblical themes. It is noteworthy that with the coming of the industrial revolution and the consequent changes in land use, so landscape painting suddenly appeared.

As a professional painter and community arts worker, I have become very unsure of what an artist is, if it is not each and every one of us. In our struggle towards autonomy, we are reminded through psychology that creativity is an instinctive behaviour in mankind and necessary for human health and well-being. Why have we overlooked it or stifled it to such a degree? Even now, contemporary education too often teaches us to be 'right', thus implying, or stating, that we may be 'wrong'. Rather than right and wrong, we need to find ways of relating to difference (both differences within ourselves and outside of ourselves) which I believe is essential if we are to move from a competitive society to a co-operative one.

What does it mean to relate to difference? It is a process – a process of questioning, probing with mind and listening and feeling with heart, allowing – or daring – our creative imagination to flow beyond discomfort. With these elements engaged, we provide fertile ground for the growth of compassion within.

To award space and time to our creativity, in a non-judgemental atmosphere, is an activity akin to prayer and contemplation. It is to say our relationship to the Divine Creator is important. It leaves us changed. Working in this way within a group means both an individual and a common journey of discovery; we learn from ourselves and each other; everyone takes an active part in our explorations.

Why painting?

Symbols and images are pre-verbal: in psychological jargon,

they are primary source materials, as are dreams. We all know the difficulty of describing dreams in words, despite the image being very vivid. Because verbalization is our principal mode of communication, from an early age we become adept at manipulating and controlling words. This tends to pre-empt imagination. By perhaps five years old, we are fairly able to say the 'acceptable' thing.

Most of us do not have the same level of guarded sophistication with drawing. It is interesting to note that in common with other professional painters who can draw, say, figures in perspective, I find that when dealing with unconscious material, my drawings become naive and childlike. Blake's visionary work has this same quality.

Spontaneous drawing and painting opens the door for each of us to encounter our unconscious self, always containing as it does both conscious and unconscious material. People often express surprise at an image – 'I don't know where *that* came from!' – whilst at the same time becoming aware that it could only have arisen from some hidden part of themselves or, equally important, from something external which for some reason has meaning for the unconscious. In this way, a picture is often a leading edge to insight, forming a bridge to oneself, thus allowing the painter to recognize the energy the image holds; to own and finally integrate it. 'What was once only imagined is now proved'.

An image may also be shocking. In the wider world, we need to move towards co-operation; this is also true within ourselves vis-à-vis our shadow side. Jung writes, 'The shadow personifies everything that the subject refuses to acknowledge about himself and yet is always thrusting itself upon him directly or indirectly – for instance, inferior traits of character and other incompatible tendencies.'[3]

Encountering an aspect of the shadow, which happens when we use symbols and images, is to risk meeting the stranger within. (Margaret Goodall refers to this in her writing on creating spaces.) Indeed, in personal terms, 'the stranger' is our untapped potential for wisdom and love. To be whole we need to risk inviting him in. 'Often, often, often, goes the Christ in the Stranger's guise' (*The Rune of Hospitality*).

The non-linear and spatial nature of pictures enables us to portray relationships all at once, which is much closer to the truth of how we experience life. This is especially pertinent when a particular issue is presented or arises from investigation, whether working individually or with a group working on a combined piece. (For example, a youth group examining 'what it means to be eighteen and living in the world today'; a community group exploring the theme, 'celebrate our differences'; an elderly group looking at 'needs, fears and the good things of being who I am'). By working together, the group is able to spiral inwards and to penetrate an issue on a very profound level, where everyone's contribution is realized and drawn in (no pun intended!). The quality of attentiveness and involvement can be quite extraordinary as the group works its way through to greater clarity and resolution. First of all we find the stillness within, and then work from a focused creative imagination. We soon see how, as the group grows in trust and confidence with themselves and each other, the activity has the quality of contemplation.

Symbols

Symbols are commonly accepted as being natural, organic modes of psychic expression, the natural language of the unconscious. They arise spontaneously, living and personified aspects of the psyche, charged with numinosity, dynamism. They produce consequences:

> A symbol represents and is also part of a larger whole. It throws together what is known and what is (as yet)

196

unknown . . . (it) discloses (however dimly) new levels of meaning both in the external world and in the personal psyche. It is a bridge that joins 'inside' and 'outside', whilst retaining a distinction.[4]

According to Paul Tillich, every symbol opens up a level of reality for which non-symbolic speaking is inadequate. But in order to do this, something else must be opened up – namely, levels of the soul, levels of our interior reality. And they must correspond to the levels in exterior reality which are opened up by a symbol. So, says Tillich, every symbol is two-edged. It opens up reality and it opens up the soul.

Colour

Colour is a vital force and an integral part of our lives. Does not everyone have an individual relationship to colour? Down through history philosophers and artists have referred to colour as the language of the soul: Goethe calls colour 'the suffering of the light', and goes on to say, 'Light and darkness are continually struggling with each other . . . as soon as its [the light's] direct effect ceases, darkness demonstrates its power in the form of shadow, twilight and night.'[5]

Colour perspective arises and sensitivity grows with use; we discover the colours as space-creating entities, they acquire gestures and expressions, we reach for a certain colour perhaps without being conscious of why. Each spot of colour speaks of something essential to us. Blue always withdraws, red presses forward, green inclines to harmony, yellow wants to dance and stimulate.

As we grow in consciousness, so more colours become visible to our physical eyes. Equally, there is nothing magical about being able to sense colour through our fingers. Many blind or near-blind people I have worked

197

with have learned this sensitivity, hardly being aware that they have substituted ways of perceiving.

Using colour is a soul experience; when working with blue, for example, a group who 'know' nothing of colour theory will tend to become quieter and quieter until eventually they begin to ask for red. Many hospitals are now using colour more consciously, whether it be red/blue/red light with a coma patient or simply using yellow in convalescent wards. This fascinating and dynamic field of research cannot be elaborated here. Suffice it to say that colour affects us powerfully; in colour we live and move and have our being.

Conclusion

Is there a relevance that this creative inward and outward moving through colour, image and symbol can offer to the wider debate? The painter, or the group, selects often unconscious material from external and internal reality, from what is known and what is present but unknown. The picture embodies a conjunction between the two. This gives an opportunity for reconciliation and resolution. It challenges our attentiveness, invites us to use the past in our understanding of now and to find our way into the future. It is as relevant to five year olds working with myth, parable and fairy tale as it is to ninety-five year olds sharing their wisdom and addressing their unfinished business, and as it is to those in mid-life investigating the complexities and issues of living responsibly and responsively in the world today. It requires no special abilities or disabilities. An activity may be confidential, deliberately and specifically therapeutic, shared by two people; celebratory, outward-moving, as shared by hundreds at the Creation Festival in Salisbury in May 1990; or used for worship by a few. The group involved might come together on a weekly or occasional basis, or may gather to work through a particular issue which everyone shares, or to produce a specific end-product. Painting may be linked with other disciplines; it works particularly well in conjunction with drama and music. The art and drama presentations at the World Wildlife Fund Festival of the Environment at Canterbury in 1989 are a good example of this.

The possibilities in practice are limitless. What is essentially important about this activity is that it produces a universal language which everyone is able to speak; it is a way of bringing to birth a deeper self-consciousness, a more profound sense of meaning, a greater response to others and to community and so, outwards and onwards, a wider relationship to this planet and ultimately, to a deeper realization of God.

What are some specific possible results on a personal level? The following benefits are listed in no order of importance:

1 Investigate inner conflicts and contradictions
2 Discover meaning
3 Catharsis, healing
4 Insight, self-awareness, reflection
5 Work with the shadow, meet the 'stranger' within
6 Express feelings and emotions
7 More profound awareness of the deep mystery of God
8 Safe way to say the unsayable
9 Ordering of experience, visually and verbally
10 Spontaneity
11 Balance left/right brain thinking, masculine and feminine, logic and emotion
12 Relaxation, fun, play
13 Increased energy and vitality
14 Freedom to make decisions, to experiment, to test out ideas
15 Confidence-building

16 Self-validation; everyone works in their own way
17 Realization of own potential
18 Increase sensitivity to the soul language of colour
19 Vulnerability
20 Remind us of joy
21 Increased personal autonomy and motivation, develop as an individual
22 Letting go of other people's expectations

On a group and community level, we may see some of the following results:

1 Greater awareness, recognition and appreciation of others
2 Move from competitiveness to co-operation, involvement in group activity
3 Communication
4 Sharing problems, insights, experiences
5 Discovery of universality of experience
6 Appreciation of uniqueness of individuals
7 Safe area for sharing and celebrating difference
8 Relating to others, understanding of effect of self on others and relationship
9 Support
10 Nurturing
11 Trust
12 Cohesion of group
13 Breaks down barriers: social, class, age, situation
14 Raise awareness of deeper and hidden concerns of group/community
15 Explore and examine issues pertinent to community
16 Problem solving
17 Group decides boundaries and ground rules
18 Acquire expertise as a group in new way of communicating
19 Learning from each other
20 Shared power and responsibility

21 Everyone can find their own level
22 Creation of community space
23 Can address itself specifically to local action or wider vision
24 The whole is greater than the sum of its parts

Appendix:
Three Examples of
Actual Painting Events

There is no such thing as a typical session. These are simply examples of events which I have conducted. Events are always organic. They grow into themselves in response to the people and their needs; therefore I do not impose any predetermined structure, but use listening skills, intuition, imagination and experience to assist the group. Despite this, I prepare a great range of possibilities (which gives me the confidence to then abandon them!). If I know something of the group in advance, and what they have in common, then it helps me to prepare ways which may help them to feel at ease. For example, all are working through mental illness; all are aged between five and ten; all are church members; all live in a certain community; all are terminally ill.

Generally there is an opening, a central process, and a closing. If we are working individually, we create regular opportunities to come together and share as a group. The exceptions to this are at drop-in/drop-out sessions, for example at the Creation Festival where some stopped by for thirty minutes, others for three hours, or three days!

People need to be able to express themselves in different ways, so I try and provide as wide a range of materials as possible, such as paint, clay, collage, pastels, charcoals, papers, and sponges, as well as 'junk' materials – such as cardboard, newsprint and plastics. If it is appropriate, I use music when we are working – also story-telling, circle dancing, poetry, singing, role playing, games etc.

Events can take place in all kinds of situations. I have worked in churches, marquees, halls, outdoors, institutions, convents, schools, stately homes, conference centres, barns, hospitals, private houses . . . and once or twice in rooms geared for artwork! I always prepare the working area very carefully. As people arrive and take their seats, everything each painter requires is to hand. Paints (liquid and clean) must look as appetising to the soul as good food to the palate. As I see it, this is part of the nurturing and service by which the arts worker sets the scene.

Example One

Youth Issues

This was a three-hour session of nine seventeen to nineteen year olds already known to each other. The group came together to present a programme for the Religious Broadcasting Department of the BBC. The emphasis was on a group exploration of issues which concerned them in the world today. The themes they felt most strongly about and chose to explore were oppression, hunger, water, and conservation. They wanted to combine artwork with drama to communicate their feelings and thoughts.

After discussion on ways and means, the group decided to split up into four smaller groups, each of these addressing themselves to one of the issues. The groups chose to work the three hours without a formal break. They used mostly paint and collage; one area became a 'hunting ground' for images. Everyone spread out and worked on the floor, each group producing a picture measuring about six feet by four feet. I sensed a growing feeling of hopelessness and impotence, pain and anger about many of the symbols and images used. Was this reflective of their own feelings?

At the end of this time, we retired to the pub to discuss the experience. The group felt pretty dismal. I challenged them: 'What's the possible positive side to all this pain you have portrayed, all this knowledge you have? Do you have to leave it at that? If not, what do you want to do about it?'

They brightened up, decided they wanted to continue working through to some kind of resolution. How? As we sat there, the idea of making one circular mandala evolved, with light, the source of life, at the centre and man taking his proper place within the kaleidoscopic scheme of things. In the final hours of New Year's Eve, on the floor of the church, this beautiful mandala was completed with an avidity and compulsion which recognized each person's longing to contribute creatively to an uncertain future.

Example Two

Who am I?

This was a three-day residential retreat for twenty-two individuals in the caring professions who were previously unknown to each other. The retreat was an opportunity to assess their present situations and spend time with their whole selves. The group became a supportive therapeutic community. Each person worked at their own pace, addressing themselves to the following tasks through the production of a series of drawings, paintings, and in (4) by using the written word:

1 Where have I come from? Lifeline and history.
2 Who am I? Present life in all aspects.
   a What makes me feel threatened, vulnerable?
   b What helps, nurtures, heals?
   c What needs to be changed, so it can grow?

3 Depict a dream (or day-dream)
4 Dialogue with the dream. (See Margaret Goodall's reference to the parable of the Good Samaritan). Write down a conversation between self and an aspect of self in the dream as symbolized by character or object. As we tune into the feeling tone of a symbol it begins to talk with us if we allow it. Ask:
    a Where do you come from?
    b What do you want from me?
    c What do you give to me?
5 Working with the positives in the negatives:
    a What drains my energy?
    b Why do I repeat it?
    c What is the pay-off for me in perpetuating it?
6 Looking to the future, collecting everything together, what do I wish for myself?

This was a very intense, concentrated event and although the group was not using words very much, the atmosphere hummed with a powerful empathy of purpose. People grew very close. In the final session there was an opportunity for those who wished to share their experiences; many were not yet ready to put anything into words, but there was much nodding of heads amidst the smiles – and shocks – of revelation. We ended in silence, by placing the final pieces of work in a circle and sharing a blessing, holding hands.

Example Three

Awakening Creativity

This was a one-day open event which was held in a country barn. Those present, mostly unknown to each other, included a general practitioner, a shopkeeper, two housewives, a bookbinder, an actor, a retired teacher, a systems analyst, a school pupil studying 'A' level art, a vicar's wife and an unemployed couple.

Apart from the student, no-one had painted since early school days; everyone was a little apprehensive before we began. In preparation, I had unrolled a long length of paper which covered everyone's tables.

After introductions and a meditation, I put on some music and everyone began to paint on the large paper, whatever the music suggested to them. After a few moments, we began to link up our work with the person's next to us, and across the table. We ended by sharing feelings about the activity. There was much relief to discover there was no judgment involved, only the experience of process!

Then we worked in pairs to make a painting, without talking, in the following ways:

1 Both working at once
2 Different partners, taking turns
3 Different partners, taking turns with the definite idea of creating something by responding to each other to make a cohesive whole.

This exercise is about becoming conscious of the ways in which we relate to and use space and territory, and how we respond to each other. This group was disarmingly honest; although doing this was serious enough, there was also much shared laughter as people admitted to feelings of anger and threat when, for example, their partner first 'poached' onto 'their territory'. Almost everyone enjoyed best the third co-operative effort.

Then, working separately, we painted quickly in response to five different kinds of music/sound. Afterwards, everyone placed their pictures in a grid pattern on the floor, thus discovering the universality of colour language. Buoyant music brought a predominance of yellows and oranges, whilst the sound of water running awakened greens and blues. One of the housewives constantly took a colour-balancing role, giving us all food for thought and discussion.

The next exercise was an opportunity to tune into the essence of natural objects, a meditative sensitizing to different life forms. The painters were encouraged not to look *at* natural objects such as seashells, plants, fruits, gemstones, seeds, eggs, but rather to paint from imaginative creativity, as if they were experiencing the object from the inside. By this stage of the day, confidence was flowing and creative imagination flowering. The atmosphere was reverent. Some extraordinarily beautiful pictures were made: an orange pip full of sunshine, imprinted with past and future blossoming of tree; an amethyst slow-growing over aeons of time, a cool and healing cave buried deep; a small crab-shell revealing the drama of life on the sea floor. As people made their pictures and then shared their experience of this task, so it awoke compassion and deeper awareness for these other forms of life, and showed us the power of insightful imagination when employed in this contemplative way.

To close, we shared a guided meditation, followed by painting the gift or quality which emerged: a tangible image of the inner stillness to carry away.

Notes

1. R. A. Assagioli, *Psychosynthesis* (Turnstone 1965).
2. The wounded healer theme relates to the mythology of Chiron. Its meaning is: 'If I can face my wounds and work towards healing, then I am better prepared to help another face and heal his/her own wounds'. We can never accompany another person beyond where we have travelled ourselves.

3. C. G. Jung, *Archetypes and the Collective Unconscious*, Collected Works, vol. 9 (Routledge 1959), p. 284.
4. R. F. Hobson, *Forms of Feeling* (Routledge 1990).
5. J. W. von Goethe, *Farbenlehre*, published in English as 'Approach to Colour' by the Society of Metaphysicians in 1988.

Index

211

Index

Orthodox Church; World Council of Churches

Church of England: Archbishop's Commission on Rural Areas 14, 122-4; Board of Social Responsibility 14; Church Commissioners 121; General Synod 68; reports 52, 72, 85, 122-4, 161-2, 164

classical Greek thought (on human nature) 29-30

Cobb, John 13

collective values 31, 32

colour 197-8

Common Ground 186

communication 140, 175; *see also* discussion; language; literature; relationships

community arts 8-9, 176-90; books 183; catalysts and stimuli 188-9; celebration 181; common factors 178; drama 178-9, 182; environmental projects 186-8; expert opinion 179; fundraising 183; local roots 188; music 182; process and product 179-80; relationships 178; rural rides or town trails 181; scale 188; scrap-books 182; sculpture 183-6

community relationships 42-4, 175-7, 189-90

consciousness 89, 93, 96, 99

Conservative Party 37

consumer religion 104-7, 109

consumerism 40, 97

Cooper, Tim 7, 121-2

cosmic Christ 90, 92-3, 94-5, 96, 97-8, 100, 114

Cotter, Jim 139

Council for the Protection of Rural England (CPRE) 18

Creation Festival, Salisbury 198, 203

creation narratives (Genesis) 39-40, 48, 50, 69-71, 90, 124

creation spirituality 5, 36, 93

creativity 194, 206-8

Cupitt, Don 105

death 38-9, 40

discussion, space for 8, 133, 134-8, 140-6, 151-2, 155, 170, 173 n.1

domination 41-2, 51, 74, 75-7, 91, 109, 110; *see also* dominion

dominion 90-1, 130 n.15

drugs 113-14

Eastern Europe 8, 136-7, 168

Eckhart, Meister 107

ecological implications of 'stewardship' concept 77-82

ecstasy 113-14, 150

Eliot, T. S. 135

Elliott, Charles 62

Ellul, Jacques 24

Enlightenment, the 7, 123

environmental organisations 3, 4, 14, 16-18, 20-1, 23, 27, 29, 47

212